WRENCH IN THE SYSTEM

WRENCH
IN THE SYSTEM

WHAT'S SABOTAGING YOUR BUSINESS SOFTWARE
AND HOW YOU CAN RELEASE THE POWER TO INNOVATE

HAROLD HAMBROSE
With a Foreword by Dan Boyarski

WILEY

JOHN WILEY & SONS, INC.

COPYRIGHT © 2009 BY HAROLD HAMBROSE. ALL RIGHTS RESERVED.
ART DIRECTOR: HAROLD HAMBROSE
BOOK AND JACKET DESIGN: SAL NISTICO
ILLUSTRATIONS AND DIAGRAMS: RUSLAN KHAYDAROV
PUBLISHED BY JOHN WILEY & SONS, INC., HOBOKEN, NEW JERSEY.

For general information on our other products and services, or technical support, please contact our Customer Care Department within the United States at 800–762–2974, outside the United States at 317–572–3993 or fax 317–572–4002.

Wiley also publishes its books in a variety of electronic formats. Some content that appears in print may not be available in electronic books.

For more information about Wiley products, visit our Web site at http://www.wiley.com.

Library of Congress Cataloging-in-Publication Data:
Hambrose, Harold, 1967-
    Wrench in the system : what's sabotaging your business software and how you can release the power to innovate / Harold Hambrose.
        p. cm.
    Includes bibliographical references and index.
    ISBN 978-0-470-41343-2 (cloth)
    1. Management information systems–Evaluation. 2. Business–Computer programs–Evaluation.
3. Business–Software–Evaluation. 4. Information technology–Management. I. Title
    HD30.213.H353 2009
    358.4′038011–dc22
                                                                                    2009010847

Printed in the United States of America
10 9 8 7 6 5 4 3 2 1

To my collaborators in the continuous and iterative design of a life:
JOHANNA, HENNEY WESTCOTT, AND **SMITH SOPHIA**

CONTENTS

FOREWORD

Business software is everyone's business: We rely on it to regulate distribution of electrical power, operate 911 lines, and store our medical records. How well these electronic tools are designed—whether they seem self-evident or whether they send ambiguous messages that cause delays and errors—can often be a matter of life or death.

Despite dazzling achievements in technology, our electronic business systems are not nearly as good as they should be. Business software is often unpredictable, unreliable, and unproductive. This is a systemic problem that causes billions of dollars in lost productivity for American businesses every year.

Successful businesses are good at solving problems, and whether a business is dedicated to providing goods or services, the process of problem solving starts with people. When one starts with questions about people's needs, instead of what technology is available or what manufacturing process should be used, then the process of developing and designing a product or a service is markedly different. This human-centered approach can be applied to almost any problem, because when we start with people and attempt to understand their true (and latent) needs in the context of their everyday lives, the answers often will reveal themselves naturally.

More often than not, the problems that plague a high-tech system are caused not by technical glitches but by miscommunication—the failure to build a clear communications link between technology and the men and women who use it. This is not a failure of technology, but an absence of the traditional process of design that solves problems by focusing on people.

Ask most anyone to explain what *design* means to them, and they'll point to a cell phone, a car, a chair—a physical artifact that they use or aspire to own. To them, design is a *noun*, something they can touch and hold. But design is also a *verb*, which suggests a specific process over a specific period of time. It is this process of problem solving, in fact, that distinguishes one designer from another, one company from another, and one designed artifact from another. A designer's most valuable skills are in problem seeking and definition, audience understanding and empathy, the exploration and refinement of form, and, probably most important, cross-disciplinary collaboration.

Recently, the press has extended its coverage of design to articles about better search engines, poorly designed ballots, back-saving ergonomic chairs, and new communications devices. What is also beginning to emerge, in the popular press as well as in business and design journals, is an understanding that designers are most valuable when they work with experts from other disciplines such as marketing, strategy, sociology, language, human factors, and engineering. Designers ask questions that get to the heart of what the problem really is, they explore a range of ideas before narrowing it down to one, and they find appropriate ways of bringing their client and their audience into the process of designing, as co-designers.

Good designers have the ability to translate and mediate between disciplines, helping a team stay focused or try a new approach. The lines between designer, client, and audience are sometimes blurred in an effort to bring new thinking to the process. An adept designer knows how to open up the process, all the while aware of where the project is on a time line, shepherding it along behind the scenes. This collaboration offers a range of perspectives, vital in dealing with today's ill-defined problems, as well as a unique opportunity for new ways of working, where hierarchical and silo-driven structures give way to flatter and more open organizations.

If cross-disciplinary collaboration and flatter organizational structures are the future, it's remarkable how many companies are still firmly grounded in the past. A close look at companies around the world reveals structure and makeup that are surprisingly similar to old manufacturing models. Change is difficult, expensive, and a threat to the status quo. But those companies that have succeeded in the face of global economic turmoil have demonstrated new ways of working across disciplines. Old models have given way to new ways of thinking about solving problems, whatever their size and complexity. Disciplines that would not have spoken to each other in the past are now working together.

Here are true stories of people and projects that illustrate this new thinking and the actions that follow. Harold Hambrose has transformed the operations of many Fortune 500 companies by showing them new ways to collaborate, to innovate, and to find low-cost design solutions to some of their most expensive problems. With insight based on highly specialized experience, he shows that design is at the crossroads of strategic thinking and problem solving.

Today, more than ever, balancing technology with human-centered solutions is requisite thinking for every executive, manager, technologist, and engineer—because design can solve problems that technology can't crack.

DAN BOYARSKI
Professor, School of Design
Carnegie Mellon University

PREFACE

When I told my parents that I wanted to study art in college, they were concerned, *After four years, would I have enough skills to support myself?* Against the advice of my high school guidance counselor, who recommended that I pursue something more professional and leave creative pastimes to the weekends, I applied to the design school at Carnegie Mellon University and chose a course of study in graphic design, which sounded more business-oriented than painting or sculpture. At that point in my life, my understanding of design was not well enough formed for me to even guess at the possibilities that lay ahead; I envisioned a career in advertising, assembling images, letterforms, and colors on the printed page just so in order to persuade someone to buy something, think something, or even feel something.

At that time, design students didn't routinely collaborate with students in the school of computer science, but members of the design faculty were wondering why not and thinking about the role that design might have in technology. They began to ask us, *What if you were designing information? What if that information changes and moves?*

During my senior year, Carnegie Mellon arranged for the technology company NCR Corporation, which had begun business in the nineteenth century by making cash registers, to sponsor a design project to explore new uses for technology, and I was one of eight students chosen to participate. NCR wanted us to consider the question of what might be different about information that moves from the printed page to a computer screen that people could manipulate. NCR challenged each of us to design a business transaction that could be conducted on a public touch screen; it was up to us to imagine what that transaction would be. This was in the spring of 1989, when relatively few people owned personal computers and most business was done by phone, by fax, by mail, or in person.

The question that NCR posed was very broad, so each of us had a different answer. One of my classmates designed an interactive system for ordering floral arrangements, with images of flowers that you could drag across the screen and drop into a pot. I was interested in real estate because I'd worked summers at my cousin's title agency, helping to prepare paperwork for settlement, so I created a plan for a kiosk with a touch screen that would let prospective home buyers browse residential properties in their area. That capability didn't exist then.

As part of the design process, our project required that we make prototypes, but the interactive software we needed wasn't widely available. Our professor, Dan Boyarski, contacted a small company that specialized in developing software for video games, a start-up outfit in Chicago called MacroMind (which later became Macromedia, now part of Adobe). Boyarski coaxed MacroMind into letting us use an early version of one of its programs and gave each of us a key to a locked room in the College of Fine Arts where the software was installed on eight computers with tiny color monitors. Then we planned, sketched, programmed, tested, designed prototypes, and retested each element of our projects.

To find out what features are most important to home buyers, I talked with real estate agents and homeowners. Then I began to make drawings, paper prototypes of page views that I showed to a small group of homeowners. With their help, I reorganized the information into a program that buyers could use to search by region, price range, and number of bedrooms and bathrooms, with options to view exterior and interior photographs as well as floor plans. Once I'd managed to program a prototype, I persuaded a group of homeowners on campus to test it and to identify areas that needed improvement.

At the conclusion of the semester, when my classmates and I presented our projects, we saw that our sponsors weren't nearly as interested in our results as in finding out how we had arrived at them. They wanted to see our sketchbooks. They asked us, *What was your process? How did you find out whether people would want a system like yours? How did you test whether people would be able to use it? Did you have the tools you needed to prototype your project the way you wanted? How often did you check the technology? Have you used the limits of existing technology?*

This experience taught me that design—the process of analyzing, sketching, prototyping, testing, and refining—can be used to solve problems far beyond the printed page, and I decided to seek employment within technology.

Persuading software developers that a newly minted graphic designer was relevant to their efforts was no simple task. The prevailing viewpoint in the technology industry was that graphic designers could make a contribution during the final stage of the development process by creating the lines, forms, and colors that can be seen on the screen. This view was absurdly narrow, but it provided a door of opportunity just wide enough for me to squeeze in my foot.

Before completing my degree, I was invited to fly to Dallas–Fort Worth for a day of interviewing at IBM's nearby Westlake campus. It soon became clear that if I were to be hired, I needed to possess programming skills of a certain caliber—skills I didn't have. At one point during my tour of the facility, a sympathetic recruiter asked me to quickly step into an elevator to avoid an approaching testing coordinator, an individual responsible for verifying the programming skills of all applicants. So I hid. And I was hired—as an independent contractor. A graphic designer didn't fit any of IBM's job classifications, and if I were to contribute to the company's efforts, it would be under my own banner.

IBM's programmers welcomed me to their team with expressions that told me that they thought they needed a designer like a fish needs a bicycle. How could they not see the importance of design to their work? Their tradition of working in isolation within the industry seemed unnatural, and the products of their labors—visible only as awkward-looking displays of data fields and obtuse word choices—were so cumbersome that I thought surely the value of my contributions would be quickly recognized. I was wrong. This experience would play itself out hundreds of times in the years ahead. With each experience I would find myself no less surprised at the missed opportunity and the unintended consequences.

It seemed obvious that ultimately the programmers' lack of concern for an individual's experience in using their software would sabotage their products, but I realized that I would have to demonstrate the value of design to the software development process. I knew that this could be done, and I began to dream of assembling a team of designers and technologists in a company of my own. At that point I wasn't thinking about designing mobile technologies or corporate dashboards or electronic health records—these things weren't in common use—and it would be more than three years before I opened an office for Electronic Ink in the United States and hired the company's first employee. In the meantime I decided that I would try to conquer this new world of technology one programmer at a time, by showing how software can benefit from traditional design processes that have been practiced for centuries.

Most successful products are developed through collaboration between designers and technologists. Designers have left their fingerprints on everyday objects throughout the history of technological advancement, from the evolution of the locomotive's form to the ever-diminishing size of portable music players. Yet for all the visual style that design has brought to our everyday experiences, designers make only marginal contributions when they recalibrate the shape of a desktop monitor or apply vibrant colors to cell phones, embellishing objects whose soul already has been defined.

Designers make their most valuable contributions when they participate in the very invention of a human being's experience with a specific object or environment, by designing a handle that is easier to grasp or an electronic tool that speeds up a business process. Designers are problem solvers and communicators. They use research, observation, and testing to find out what problems a product needs to solve for the people who use it, and when they partner with technology they can create innovative solutions that exceed our expectations. A graphic designer for an automotive company can convert an engineer's calculation of a dangerously low oil level into a warning light on the dashboard; an architect can express a client's requirements for a corporate headquarters with specifications that greatly exceed the need for shelter; and a designer can shape complex software that is as easy to use as an ATM. But many so-called software designers are technologists, not designers, and a technologist's first loyalty is to the code, not to the customer.

Designers specialize in collaborating with professionals in other disciplines in order to create strong connections between products and the people who use them. To be fully effective, a designer needs to be present at the creation of a product, participating in its development from the start and bringing to the process an understanding of how people will use it. A designer who arrives on the scene at the end of the software development process will be limited to creating an aesthetic effect for a set of predetermined words and images that may not make sense to their audience.

The corporate research and development labs that produce luxury automobiles, iPods, and easy-to-use search engines such as Google have learned that innovation and advancement are the result of a process of analysis, experimentation, collaboration, and consensus among such diverse disciplines as computer science, psychology, anthropology, engineering, and design. Unfortunately, when it comes to the software that drives business, manufacturers have developed some bad habits over the past 30 years: an indifference to classic design processes, a focus on features, and a lack of concern for the people who might benefit most from those features (if only they fully understood how to use them). As a result, the software industry offers an enormous selection of powerful electronic tools that disappoint those who buy them and frustrate those who use them because their value compares so poorly with their cost.

American businesses spend billions of dollars on electronic systems to drive every aspect of their operations, from accounts receivable to global production and delivery schedules, yet many of these systems are unwieldy or even unworkable. Business owners have become conditioned to buying this technology reluctantly, anticipating that any new system will be difficult to implement; their employees, whose individual productivity is influenced by the quality of the software they use, have come to regard each upgrade warily. Too often, instead of achieving promised gains in savings and productivity, companies are confronted by low rates of user adoption, unexpected training costs, and maintenance and support tasks that are difficult if not impossible to perform.

Software developers have attempted to address the issue of design through a myriad of ineffective channels. For years human factors professionals have provided laboratory settings in which to test developing software for usability. Like closing the barn door after the horses are out, these tests usually examine expensive developing software at a stage when it's not likely to be substantially changed, regardless of the feedback from usability tests. Designers themselves have ineffectively tried to provide how-to manuals to industry, explaining techniques and best practices to be applied to every step of the software development process. These manuals read well, and they may serve to heighten awareness of design's value, but they all read like recipes in a cookbook—precise measures of ingredients using utensils that may not quite match the ones you have on hand and that may not produce the result you expect, even when you follow directions to the letter. A cookbook is no substitute for the knowledge and technique of an experienced cook or a master chef who can advise you on how to substitute an ingredient, how to adjust the quantity of the finished dish to suit your needs, or how to compensate for influences such as high altitude and humidity. No cookbook can describe all the exceptions to every guideline, and a software manual is no substitute for designers and the design process.

The disparity between the immense power of business software and its weak performance can be resolved, but the answer can't be found in technology. The source of the problem is a broken connection between technology and the people who use it. Executives of both business and technology cling to a flawed development process that is limited to making an assessment of business needs, specifying what a system must do, and constructing software products with little consideration of how they will work in the hands of human beings.

The less a buyer knows about a product, the riskier the purchase. Making a big bet on information technology means just that: Typically, before anyone in a company has an opportunity to see the software as the staff will see it every day, the check is signed. Often, business owners place their confidence in a requirements document or purchase order that lists only the tasks and transactions to be supported by a system. Some executives demand to know the training requirements of a new system early on, but they seldom see their new software as it will appear on the screen until a substantial portion of the development budget has been consumed and project momentum precludes anyone from insisting on a review stage that threatens to slow progress toward the delivery deadline.

Successful software development is much more than a triumph of programming. At its most effective, the process is similar to the design, specification, and construction of a building, in which an architect collaborates and communicates with both the client and the contractors. As with the creation of a building, engineering is only one set of skills required to design and develop successful software. Specialized business expertise also is essential, but very few business executives possess the multiplicity of skills needed to act as architect. Members of other disciplines are needed to communicate with the men and women who use the software on a daily basis and to provide essential information about how they interpret visual signals, how they learn, and what they are most likely to remember.

When designers participate in the software development process, they may enlist the expertise of linguists who can suggest words that people easily recognize, cartographers who can map a route through a maze of data, architects who can visualize information in three dimensions, and psychologists who can predict what will cause most people to make a mistake. Designers and technologists who collaborate to build on this information can forge a strong link between the product and the people who use it, and they can design something that is just as important as the software itself: They can design the experience of using it.

Software that is easy to use benefits everyone. It gives people the freedom to turn their attention from the task to the goal, and it gives organizations a competitive advantage by lowering training costs and raising productivity. Although the true quality of software is invisible until it is put to use, its performance can be tested and measured like any other product, and its success can be seen in the way it speeds its users to their destinations.

There's no reason that most business software can't be as easy to use as driving a car. What's needed is a development process that has the power to revolutionize a young industry whose greatest achievements are just ahead.

ACKNOWLEDGMENTS

I came to understand design through a series of encounters that would build on one another—each revealing a new facet of this discipline, and each asking me to further apply my understanding to new and unexpected challenges. For the foundation of my design training and indeed my understanding of this field today, I will forever be in the debt of Carnegie Mellon University's College of Fine Arts and its Department of Design: Mary Weidner and Mark Mentzer, who taught me first how to see, and then how to draw; Charlee Brodsky, Karen Moyer, Stephen Stadelmeier, and Todd Cavalier, who planted in me the kernel of design—an understanding of composition, form, and appreciation for the audiences I would serve throughout my career; and Dan Boyarski, who encouraged me to push design and its immense value to new areas of the business landscape and to challenge the software industry that has much to gain through the power of design.

Along the way many corporate leaders allowed me to test the ideas presented in this book within their businesses: IBM's Tony Temple; Columbia University's Leon Gold; Ingres' Roger Burkhardt; Anne Wilms and Tony D'Alessandro at Rohm and Haas Chemicals; SEI Investments' Al West and Judy Tschirgi; First Data Corporation's

Tom Hurley; Deutsche Bank's Tony Pizi; Penske's Brian Hard; Denis Weil at McDonald's; Lincoln Financial's David Wozniak; Microsoft's Andrew Kirby; PJM Interconnection's Ken Huber; Bloomberg's Shawn Edwards; Wyeth's Kris Jackson; Dick Proctor at MBNA Bank; Cat Callo at Reuters; Princeton Financial System's Charlie Morris; Sun Life's Priscilla Brown; and Mercer's Rick Lindbergh.

Through the doors of Electronic Ink, many brilliant professionals have walked. All of these people have challenged our past successes and have broken new ground through tireless commitment to design innovation: David Rode, Jim Girgenti, Sue Patten, Sal Nistico, Gerianne Bartocci, Sagan Medvec, Ruslan Khaydarov, Donamarie Schettino, Steve Williams, Tracy Kroop, Tony Daddario, Michael McAghon, Mark Ziegler, Nefeli Stavrinidi, Andy Stopani, Jim Ross, Kevin Richardson, Jim Morris, Max Snyder, Devon Keller, Paul Nuschke, James Temple, Rob Tannen, Nadine Fox, Ryan Caplan, Aaron Martlage, and Shushi Yoshinaga.

Picture research for this publication was skillfully carried out by Susan Oyama.

Jackie Whyte managed thousands of details and ensured that this project ran according to plan.

For so thoughtfully reviewing the manuscript and bringing important insights and observations to this project, thanks to Julian Hirst and Clare Cotugno.

I am grateful to my consulting editor, Nancy Steele, for her talent, focus, and friendship. Her insight and expertise were essential to the development of this book.

Michael Friedman understood the value of this book and supplied an energized and creative plan for its publication.

The terrific team at John Wiley & Sons, especially Tim Burgard, Andrew Wheeler, and Stacey Rivera, have given me strong support and great latitude in designing every aspect of this book—the message of its words, and the form they have taken on the page.

John, Tom, Jim, Stephanie Baloh, Chris, and Nan—my siblings—and Gerwyn Price, Simon Jones, Craig Tomlyn, and Phil Appleby, the finest friends, were my earliest sounding boards and strongest supporters.

I am forever grateful to Johanna, my partner in life and work, who left a legal career behind in order to help define Electronic Ink and raise its profile in the marketplace.

Finally, without the friendship, wisdom, and unflagging support of my partner and friend Joe Weiss, this book would never have been completed. Joe has brought the gravity of immense business experience to this project and to the endeavor of growing Electronic Ink—thank you, Joe.

ONE

IT'S JUST A PRODUCT!

Computer software is so immensely powerful, so fearsomely complex, and so deeply embedded in our daily routine that it's usually considered to be quite unlike all other consumer goods. To most of us, its workings are invisible and incomprehensible. Yet there's nothing magic about software. It's just a product—a man-made tool that is developed, manufactured, marketed, licensed, and sold.

Software has much in common with every other product, with one very important difference:

> *We have come to accept that the software we use won't work in the way we expect.*

We maintain high expectations for every major product we buy, especially when we purchase or lease any form of business equipment—except one. Our experience with information technology has taught us that whenever we plan to install new software, whether it's a basic word-processing program or a multimillion-dollar enterprise system, the most realistic viewpoint is to hope for the best and expect the worst.

Unfortunately, our low expectations concerning software products are justified. After a 10-year global survey of more than 50,000 information technology projects purchased and developed for firms both large and small, The Standish Group, a Massachusetts market research firm specializing in software, reported in 2004 that less than one-third of these projects were delivered on time, on budget, with the required features and functions. More than half of them came in late, were over budget, or lacked required features, and the remainder were canceled or never used.

We possess every resource we need to produce business technology that fulfills all its promise. By making small, low-tech adjustments to existing software systems and by changing the way we specify, evaluate, and develop new systems, we can overcome their short-comings and exponentially improve their performance—but only if we begin to change the way we think about them.

THE WORLD'S BIGGEST LEMONS

Whenever we buy a product, we have certain expectations.

If we decide to order a powerful new luxury car, we expect that all of its features will perform in a predictable way, from the steering wheel to the sound system. We have every reason to expect that this car will give us a smooth ride and an absolutely great experience. But imagine being told by the dealer that once you take delivery you should expect a period of adjustment because at first the gauges on the dashboard may seem confusing, and the steering wheel may be a little tricky to maneuver. What would you think if you researched consumer reviews of this model and found out that, overall, your chances of being satisfied with your purchase were only one in three? Would you be reassured if the dealer explained that the purchase price included the cost of sending a manufacturer's representative to ride alongside you for several hours each week to provide training? There's no question that you'd take your business elsewhere. But what if every dealer of every automotive brand in the United States and Germany and Japan told you the same thing?

Why is so much of our software so unsatisfactory? It's not for a lack of resources or planning. For most businesses, information technology is a priority that may represent their biggest investment. Highly detailed specifications for these systems are written by expert technologists in collaboration with some of the best minds in the business community, and these products are developed by brilliant technicians. Breathtaking advances in technology have become commonplace, and the business of testing software has become a $13 billion world market. Yet we still struggle to operate the software that serves our everyday needs. We greet each successive upgrade cautiously, anticipating problems with new features while hoping that old features will be easier to use; but time after time, when we face a computer screen and touch a keyboard, we find that something is amiss.

Disappointed buyers of expensive software "solutions" often find that they have little recourse. If your car turns out to be a lemon, you have strong protection under both federal and state laws. In fact, if you pay more than $25 for almost any product that doesn't work properly despite its written warranty, the Magnuson-Moss Act will back you in court, and every state has enacted the Uniform Commercial Code, which enables buyers to obtain satisfaction for goods that fail to perform according to the terms of their contracts. But standard purchase and licensing agreements for software

contain limitations on liability, so buyers of unsatisfactory software often have little recourse unless they have the foresight, the negotiating muscle, and the expertise to modify these contracts. As a result, the owner of a $15 million software product that turns out to be too difficult to use has much less chance of obtaining a refund or a replacement than the buyer of a defective DustBuster.

Is it a lemon? If it runs, it's not a lemon. (If the handling is rough—tough!)

Not even a lemon law would protect the buyer of an enterprise system that is engineered to be technically perfect but designed so clumsily that almost no one can understand how to use it. When it comes to buying software solutions, the most effective way to obtain full value from your investment is to ask the right questions.

THE CHECKLIST

Buyers of business software generally use two kinds of checklists to evaluate these new products: one for the business requirements and another for the technology.

To identify the business requirements, business owners usually make a list of all the tasks that the software needs to support, and they use that inventory as a yardstick to compare the features and functions of various software systems.

To answer questions about the technology of competing software products, the chief information officer asks:

What's the vendor's reputation?
What's the industry buzz on the vendor's platform?
What are the hardware considerations?
How does rollout happen?
How do we receive updates?
Are the updates reliable?
What kind of support does this vendor offer?

Sweet spot—
the interaction
of business,
technology,
and design

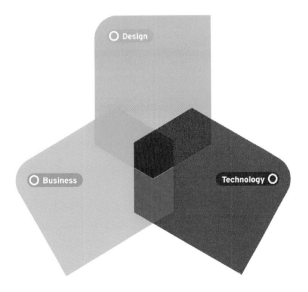

But all too often, no one asks questions that will reveal whether the software will be a good fit—whether it will do the job the way it needs to be done, whether it can be easily understood, or even whether anyone in the company will use it. Evaluating the features and functions of a well-established product from SAP, Oracle, Microsoft, or another major vendor is one thing; successfully using that product in your own company is an altogether separate activity.

A buyer's checklist needs to do far more than confirm that a software product meets every business and technical requirement; it also needs to ask how well it fulfills certain human requirements:

> *How clearly does it communicate to the people who will be using it?*
> *Is the information presented in a logical sequence?*
> *How consistent is this system?*
> *How flexible is it?*
> *How forgiving is it?*
> *What's it like to use this product?*

Technology can't answer these questions, and business analysts often overlook them. Yet this information means the difference between a system that supports efficiency and innovation and one that incurs enormous hidden costs in errors, delays, and lost opportunities.

Despite the best efforts of experts in business and technology to specify their requirements, nearly everyone recognizes that something is deeply wrong with most computer software: It works, but it seems capricious because it doesn't always work the way we think it will, and much of the time it just doesn't make sense to us. As the prison captain portrayed by actor Strother Martin famously observed in the film *Cool Hand Luke,* what we have here is failure to communicate.

FAILURE TO COMMUNICATE

The way we do our work has profoundly changed, and yet we've only begun to shape the tools we use every day.

We've become accustomed to having astonishingly powerful information technology at our disposal: Electronic systems enable us to gather, store, and share complex information with a few keystrokes. Energy traders use sophisticated software to monitor market activities and to balance supply and demand on a minute-to-minute basis.

Not getting the message— Paul Newman in *Cool Hand Luke*

Manufacturers use software to take orders, manage inventory, link assembly lines with loading docks, calculate delivery routes and schedules, and connect customers with call centers around the world, displaying each transaction in fine detail on any number of computer screens. In many hospitals, physicians use handheld computers to record information about their patients and to order diagnostic tests and medication.

The effectiveness of these tools is determined not only by the accuracy of the data and the precision of the code that drives that data, but also by how well the information is organized and how clearly it's presented on the screen. For all the millions of professionals actively engaged in utilizing information technology—whether they manage the flow of electricity, staff a customer-service hotline, or head an intensive care unit—the quality of the software they use will determine whether the process of exchanging information becomes

Billboard ads in airports across the globe boast of the relationships that bind business and technology.

a cost-effective, satisfying experience or a continuing source of errors and delay. In transportation, health care, weather forecasting, and many other sectors, this can be a matter of life or death.

By 2008, estimated annual revenues from the sale of U.S. packaged software had risen to $149 billion, a 46 percent increase from 2000, according to the U.S. Department of Commerce. Hundred-million-dollar enterprise systems and $49 personal accounting applications have become everyday wonders of technology. For individuals, these systems offer to save time and money and to provide better communications and computing capabilities; for industry, their promises of increased efficiency and a healthier bottom line make their ownership and use a necessity. But the reality of ownership often falls well short of its promise, and dramatically short of what might have been.

Often these deficiencies are only minor inconveniences, and sometimes they're even mildly amusing. One morning not long ago, my desktop printer inexplicably began to print a report in Chinese, even though the monitor in front of me displayed the text in English. Technical glitches in software are so common that we're not really surprised when something bizarre happens. But when the quality of software compromises our business, our personal privacy, or our safety, no one is amused. A $10 billion error briefly disrupted the New York Stock Exchange in 2007 when a trader for Morgan Stanley placed an order for $10.8 million of stocks. The electronic order-entry tool he was using had a built-in multiplier of 1,000, and when the system automatically raised the order to $10.8 billion, more than 81 million shares were traded before the order could be cancelled. The Exchange fined Morgan Stanley $300,000.

The volatility of supply and demand makes businesses especially vulnerable to flaws in software products that manage order processing and inventory. A famous fiasco occurred when a new computerized fulfillment system at Hershey Foods broke down in the fall of 1999, leaving retailers' shelves empty of candy just before Halloween and causing $150 million in projected sales to vanish. In 2005, a $20 million enterprise resource planning system for the medical equipment corporation Invacare caused so much disruption in order processing that the company lowered its fourth-quarter sales estimates by $30 million.

Some software bugs are potentially deadly. In Louisville, Kentucky, the city's computerized emergency dispatch system suddenly froze one evening in November 2005. Earlier that day, software for the dispatch system had been upgraded, but by about nine P.M. dispatchers were unable to disconnect 911 calls as they were completed. The lines quickly clogged, and for two hours no new callers could get through. A year earlier, at an air-traffic control center in Palmdale, California, a high-tech, touch-screen communication system shut itself down, snarling air traffic across the country until the system could be restarted three hours later. During that period at least five planes came dangerously close to one another, and 800 flights in Southern California were diverted, delayed, or canceled because controllers at Palmdale couldn't communicate with planes in the air or with other air-traffic control centers. The problem was traced to a computer program that caused communication systems at air-traffic control centers across the country to shut down unless someone manually reset them every 30 days.

The Associated Press reported in January 2009 that software glitches at the Veterans Administration (V.A.) had caused errors and delays in treatment at its medical centers around the country. Because the V.A.'s electronic system did not clearly show physicians' stop orders for medications, some patients received prolonged doses of drugs such as the blood thinner heparin, which can be fatal in excessive doses.

The full cost of the glitches, bugs, and errors in software products is unknown, but a study by the U.S. National Institute of Standards found in 2002 that software errors cost the American economy $59.5 billion annually. The effect of technical failure is immediate and clear, but technical flaws represent only part of the problem. More subtle but equally serious is the damage caused by software that is precisely engineered to perform every function, but whose users can't make it work.

Very often, even software whose performance is technically perfect seems counterintuitive. As a result, countless working systems are defeating the purposes for which they were created because they cause so much difficulty for the individuals who use them.

What if you bought a fast, powerful new car, only to discover that before you could lower the windows, view the gas gauge, or turn on the news, you had to stop the car and put it into reverse? If your dealer told you, "That's just the way it is; they're all that way," would you regard that as acceptable?

The cost of software that's hard to use is impossible to estimate, but it's a pervasive problem, and one that's at least as significant as the cost of technical flaws. In most cases, the fundamental flaw can be traced to a missing feature—lack of clear communication with human users.

BEHIND THE HYPE

The more expensive a product, the more grandiose the marketing hyperbole, and software is no exception. These sales pitches for software systems are as implausible as they are for any other product:

"Software is unlike anything else."

Although they can be very big and strong, software systems have a lot in common with every other product that is manufactured, marketed, and sold to the business community—and there's no reason they can't be made to better serve you.

"New software technology will give you a competitive edge."

Bundles of new features won't solve old problems unless they provide easier access to information within your organization. A system that is difficult to use will slow your operations and can even bring them to a standstill.

"If you fully specify your business needs, technologists can engineer the solution."

Technology can't give us all the information we need unless we specify the human requirements as well as the business requirements.

Clear communication, valuable business intelligence, and strong decision support are based on analysis and interpretation of data. To be meaningful, these processes must include information about the requirements of the people who use the technology.

"Software solutions that have been developed specifically for your industry will meet all your business needs."

How similar is your business to those of your competitors across the street, across the country, or across the ocean? Are most companies in your industry about the same size, and do they use the same work processes and share the same corporate culture? Do they even speak the same language?

Businesses are as varied as the human beings who run and staff them, and most systems will need some adjustment to fulfill the business requirements and meet the needs of the men and women who use them to do their work.

"As soon as everyone gets used to it, your system will be easy to use."

The need for intensive training is a symptom of a serious defect, and sophisticated systems often languish on desktops despite extended training programs.

Training should be an opportunity to learn how to use a business system to improve productivity, not a series of lessons in how to manipulate the counterintuitive features of a balky tool.

"If your software system isn't delivering the results you want, you need an upgrade, and you may want a customized system."

Even an old legacy system may be a technological wonder that just needs to be taught to speak English.

Low-tech, low-cost changes such as clarifying language, simplifying access codes, creating shortcuts, reordering sequences, submerging marginal functions, removing irrelevant features, and eliminating visual clutter can have a big payoff. The bigger the system, the more flexibility you may have to tweak it, but nearly every business system can be reconfigured in small ways that can dramatically improve performance and productivity.

Before you write off your sunk costs, consider whether the system you have can be adjusted to deliver what you need.

Early adopter—my grandfather, Harold Flavell Westcott, M.D., in 1918, extracting the benefits of owning a car

THE WRENCH ON THE FRONT SEAT

The information technology available to us is as fast as the speed of light, more powerful than most of us can imagine, and as reliable as the clock ticking in the hall. But this technology doesn't serve us nearly as well as it could, simply because we do not develop software through processes that genuinely consider those who will use these products.

Today, most business software is like so much of our public transportation: uncomfortable and unpredictable, avoided by those who have the means to do so, and tolerated by those without.

A balanced perspective—my grandparents, Harold and Grace, at left, with friends

My grandfather was a surgeon who was stationed in the American Southwest with the U.S. Army during World War I, and during this time he owned a Model T. When I asked my grandmother what she remembered about that first car—was it the speed, or the freedom of the open road, or was it just the feeling of having the wind in her hair?—she told me that what she remembered most was sitting on the wrench. The car was supplied with a few basic tools, and a wrench was stored on the front passenger seat. She said that the experience that she remembered in that car was sitting on the tools.

My grandmother was something of a snob, and she also said that the car made an auto mechanic of her husband because every so many miles he had to reach underneath the hood and make adjustments with the tools that the manufacturer had supplied to him. This was regarded as normal, part of the responsibility of ownership. It was as if the manufacturer had said, "If you are going to own this technology, you are going to accept these things."

My grandmother wasn't hoping for a car that had power windows or an automatic transmission, and she wasn't expecting the car to talk to her. The only innovation she wanted was not to have the imprint of a wrench on her bottom. She was asking for just a little more comfort. Furthermore, she didn't like seeing her husband transformed from respected surgeon to amateur mechanic. This last concern cannot be underestimated, because in making decisions about the things we buy, we're strongly affected by what these things say about us and how they make us feel. And that's the level of conversation that you have today whenever you ask people about their experiences with software: The usability of the system is the proverbial wrench under everyone's bottom.

Clumsy, ineffective software makes everyone who uses it feel uncomfortable. It causes employees to perform poorly, so it gives them a negative impression of their value as workers, and it also makes a company seem unconcerned for its employees and disconnected from the needs, the expectations, and the goals of its customers.

By today's standards, the Model T was a lemon: hard to start, hard to steer, and often in need of adjustment. But long before the Model T morphed into Mustangs and Explorers, Ford began to design and engineer its products to make them more practical and more appealing to customers. Rather than adding extra padding to the seats or moving the wrench, the manufacturer eliminated the need for a readily accessible tool kit by designing a product that doesn't require constant maintenance.

Today we take it for granted that we can start a new car with the flick of a wrist and that it will give us a smooth, quiet ride, keep us warm

Dashboard data from a Mercedes at a glance and with the press of a finger

in winter and cool in summer, bring us the latest news and our favorite music, show us how to reach our destination, and even help protect us in a collision, all without requiring us to do little more than refuel or recharge it from time to time and change the oil every few thousand miles.

To design business software that we can use with the same assurance, we need to consider the history of product design and manufacturing. We need to think about how those older processes—those ways of modeling objects to suit the needs of the people who use them—can be applied to the process of building new software and modifying existing systems. Imagining these collections of features and functions to be different from all other consumer goods in the history of commerce has brought us to where we are today: We possess tremendously powerful technology, but our experience with that technology routinely makes us miserable.

INVENTING AN EXPERIENCE

Successful manufacturers of consumer goods create something more than good products. They create great experiences.

One of the multitudes of innovative and influential consumer products launched during the twentieth century was the MP1, a stylish, portable communications device created by a pioneering technology company. The company had been founded by a visionary engineer who understood the necessity for his company to adopt new technology and to respond to changes in the marketplace. He was very concerned with the physical form of his products, because he knew that an attractive form would make them more popular, and he recruited architects and designers to join his development team. The company's first products were unremarkable—manual typewriters manufactured at a small factory near Turin, Italy, that could turn out 20 machines a week. But Camillo Olivetti, who founded the company in 1908, adopted new forms of labor organization and new techniques of mass production, and the company prospered. By 1930, the company was producing 13,000 typewriters a year and had opened its first European subsidiary.

In 1932 Olivetti introduced the first portable type-writer. This handsome machine, with an innovative design by Aldo Magnielli that made the chassis inde-pendent of its frame, was the MP1. As beautiful as it was practical, the MP1 won quick acceptance. New models followed, including the Studio 42, which was designed for both home and office use, and the Lexikon 80, a manual typewriter designed in 1948 by architect Marcello Nizzoli and sheathed in enam-eled aluminum, a machine so sleek and elegant that it was added to the design collection of the Museum of Modern Art.

The MP1, the Studio 42, and the Lexikon 80 were soon succeeded by Olivetti's own electric typewriters and personal computers as the company established itself as a global leader in communications technology now known as Telecom Italia S.p.A. Yet even today these manual typewriters, long obsolete, continue to attract our admiration as iconic examples of innova-tive, practical products designed to please. This isn't the case with any software ever invented. At least, I have yet to hear anyone say, "I love my word process-ing software!"

Portable word processor:
Olivetti's MP1

When I asked my grandmother about her memories of her first car, I expected an expression of nostalgia to cross her face, but instead I saw something quite different. Try to imagine yourself many years from now, recalling the computer that now sits on your desk, remembering your experience with it, and smil-ing with satisfaction. More likely you'll react just as my grandmother did to an old photo of her Model T: "Ugh—that old thing!"

Designed to be versatile:
Olivetti's Studio 42

Olivetti's innovative typewriters were the products of a well-established process that capable businesspeople have long used to design and manufacture consumer products. That process began with a consideration of the physical form that the product would take. First a designer would make sketches and models to describe the shape and size of the product, and that proposal would be evaluated according to how well it met the needs or desires of its intended market. The next step was to test a prototype with members of its target audience, and often those tests led to revisions in the design. Once approved, the design would be refined and expressed in detailed manufacturing specifications; then, at each stage of the manufacturing process, the product would be measured for accuracy and the design would be validated, keeping in mind as a constant point of reference the relationship between the product and the consumer.

Nearly 70 years later, Apple Computer used a similar process to create its first digital music player. The iPod was developed over an eight-month period in 2001 by a team of nearly 300 designers, programmers, and engineers in the United States and India. The development team built it feature by feature, with special attention to the user interface, and when the first prototypes were built, Apple CEO Steve Jobs was among those who tested each one to see exactly how well it worked.

The iPod was visionary not only because it was smaller, more powerful, and more stylish than any other device of its kind, but also because its unique wheel made it simple to operate. The iPod was designed and engineered to be compact, capacious, elegant, and clear—so clear that a novice could easily load, locate, and play thousands of songs. This was a new object that didn't look quite like anything else, and it had impressive capabilities. But the iPod's most compelling aspect was its combination of extraordinary technology and brilliant design.

The design process moves bright ideas like the MINI Cooper from concept to commercialization.

The iPod succeeded not because it packaged great features in a new form, but because anyone could easily use those features. The iPod was so much easier to operate than its competitors, and so much more convenient to carry, that using it became a new experience. The innovation of iPod was to create something we didn't know we wanted—not only a new object, but also a new form and a new experience!—all so well executed that it became instantly desirable to people everywhere. Not only did millions of buyers find the iPod useful and attractive, but something else happened: People made it part of their daily routines. Apple reinforced this concept by marketing the iPod on its web site as "an ideal companion," and its print ads featured silhouettes of young people wearing iPods and dancing with joy. Using the iPod became an experience that nearly everyone wanted.

Easy to love—
The iPod is
designed to offer
an experience
that feels like
second nature.

iPod photo courtesy
of Apple

The iPod and the MP1 are the successful products of a traditional development process that is driven by concern for its users. However, when we consider the products of information technology, it's clear that the skills, the rigor, and the goals that drive other product companies have not effectively influenced the design and development of most software.

Developers of new business software pack their products with features, but little of this advanced technology represents any improvement in the experience of using it. More often, new software products are merely new objects—new forms, new features, or even new compilations of old features, which rely on these innovations alone for their success. Business executives consider these products highly desirable because of the increased efficiencies they promise, but those who use them typically find them less than efficient. In fact, the professionals for whom these products are intended may be unwilling or even unable to use them despite the rewards they might derive from them.

An innovative form or a new feature can go only so far to satisfy its users. Olivetti's MP1 may have boosted morale among those who used it, but its sleek design didn't make the task of typing easier or faster. In itself, the iPod is both a beautiful device and a wonderful experience: The gesture of my finger to elicit an almost magical response from the technology puts a smile on my face. The result of that interaction is a delightful experience with my music, my media—things I've chosen according to my personal taste. But this delight contrasts starkly with the scowl that I wear when I interact with the broader continuum of Apple iPod ownership—which extends to my on-screen experience with iTunes. Here, even technology's coolest music player demonstrates profound weakness in understanding how software should satisfy its end user. Managing lists, understanding the limits of this device, and making a purchase is so difficult that my 11- and 12-year-old daughters have to struggle to buy movies even though they have permission to charge them to my account. When my computer-savvy preteen daughters have so much trouble spending my money, something is wrong.

Not even Apple has fully solved the problem of how to give the people who use its products a great experience—far from it. There's no doubt that Apple makes a sexy personal computing cabinet. The company pays an exceptional amount of attention to the design of the cabinetry that encases the everyday on-screen challenges of its user population, giving us innovative shapes and CPUs incorporated into pristine boxes and monitors with shiny, rounded corners that sit elegantly on our desks—all very beautiful. But on-screen, can anyone argue that the Apple O/S experience is truly far superior to the user environment of the icon-driven Windows desktop and its maze of file directories? I have wrestled with both Apple and PC

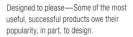

Designed to please—Some of the most useful, successful products owe their popularity, in part, to design.

iPhone 3G photo courtesy of Apple

Some of the best design is invisible.

DES|GNED

In the late 1980s I moved to New York City to work as a freelancer for one of the hot design firms at that time. This firm's work was largely print-based, but I was there to consult on the company's account with Citibank, designing what would become the customers' experience with the bank's new automated teller machines.

During my time in New York I was able to run with a lot of graphic designers and see the so-called best work of that time. What I saw the leaders of the design community calling the best was often what I called *useless:* Broadway production posters with typographic treatments that may have captured the feeling of a performance but were almost impenetrable when it came to deciphering performance times, locations, and ticket prices; product packaging with beautiful color palettes and cool imagery, but also with type that was so tiny, even my 21-year-old eyes couldn't read it.

When I discussed the problems I had recognizing these confusing creations as examples of exceptional design, many fellow designers scoffed, saying that the very characteristics that troubled me were the things that made these objects special—an expression of their designers' individual visions. *Yikes!* To me, these were the traits that ruined my experience with each object. It seemed clear that utility and quality of experience were not standard design priorities. What I believed to be an opportunity to succeed by communicating clearly, directly, and gracefully to an audience was seen by other designers as an opportunity to express their own voices.

TO D|SAPPEAR

It's said that great actors disappear into their roles. Whenever Laurence Olivier took the stage, he seemed to become the character he was portraying, masterfully presenting the playwright's vision to an audience through the use of carefully honed skills. The results for the audience were the emotions and experiences as intended by the writer, the director, the producer, and, of course, the actor.

As technology advances beyond the screen, there are enormous opportunities to design satisfying experiences with our electronic tools. Unlike icons and data fields on a computer display, much of our new technology is represented by little or no physical form. Consider the voice-activated phone system in your car: Simply press a button, and an audible prompt triggers a list of choices in your mind. This experience reflects a true understanding of the business goals that inspired this object's existence as well as the needs, expectations, and capabilities of its target audience, all orchestrated and designed into a satisfying experience with a product that is nearly invisible. In the ether of this human-machine interface, there's no place for a designer's thumbprint.

desktops and have grown equally frustrated, although for different reasons. Despite the zealous loyalty of Apple and PC partisans, each group of products exists within an environment that is miles from an end user's ideal experience—although perhaps in different directions.

In any consumer product, technology and usability are so intertwined that neither can succeed without the other. Rarely are the two elements in perfect balance, but when the developers of a product possess the will and the know-how to create an innovative form that positively influences the experience of using it, the appeal and the value of that product will be almost unlimited.

JUST WHAT WE NEED

All great products have one thing in common: They seem to be designed just for you.

Successful products appeal to the hearts and minds of the men and women who use them, and most consumer products are developed through a process of testing and evaluation that keeps the focus on humans. The software development process is very different.

The process of developing business software has been driven by priorities unlike those of traditional product design. Typically, software developers bring just two concerns to the process—the business requirements and the technology needed to execute them. Far too little thought is given to the practical problems of the people who will use these systems as many as eight hours a day, and almost no thought at all to how the knowledge and abilities of these individuals might influence the design of the software.

Many executives and software developers are convinced that if technicians can write the code to satisfy the business requirements, then the human beings who use the systems will fall in line and adapt their behavior to suit the software. (That swearing you did last time you used Microsoft Word: That was an example of what happens when you're forced to adapt your behavior to a technologist's idea of how you should be working.) Not enough consideration is given to whether these basic business tools could be more effective and more pleasing, or how these tools are affecting the relationships between employers, their customers, and their employees.

It's true that managers can accomplish great things on a large scale by persuading (or ordering) large numbers of workers to behave in a certain way. In theory, if you post identical information on a thousand computer screens in your organization, you can teach a thousand workers to consistently respond to that information in the same way. But in reality this is not going to happen, because it's just too easy for human beings to do otherwise. When the act of performing a task is as intimate as an individual sitting in front of a computer screen, with a private view of that screen, that individual has choices. He or she can choose to work quickly or slowly, to try something or not, and to be effective or ineffective. And this is where the absence of design—the inattention to human needs— becomes most noticeable and creates the greatest risk to a business investment in technology.

Software manufacturers are generally confident that their products will succeed on the strength of their technology. But products that don't appeal to their users can be self-defeating. Whenever software systems create obstacles—technical jargon, ambiguous messages, illogical sequences, or visual clutter—the people who use these systems will respond in a variety of ways.

Building software that doesn't make it possible for its users to follow a clear, straight path is like forcing drivers to navigate a succession of cloverleaf intersections and unmarked detours in order to continue along an expressway leading due north. The results will be similar: Just as some drivers will lose their way and others will cut across the median strip to seek an alternate route, those who use unsympathetic software will disobey commands whenever possible and try to find a more direct approach by navigating around the barriers. All of them will feel badly every mile of the journey, and they'll be weary and frazzled by the time they reach their destination, if they arrive at all.

Part of the process of developing software should be to identify the most appropriate route from the perspective of the user, within the constraints imposed by business and technology. It's not always possible to build highways exactly where we want them to go, and software developers often discover a conflict between what's best for a business, what best serves its customers, and what's best for the employees who will use the system. However, it's possible to find a good compromise, one that utilizes the best available technology to make a finished product that people consider to be not only valuable and but also practical and easy to use.

If a product as mundane as a wristwatch or as technologically complex as a digital music player can bring us satisfaction and pleasure because of the way they work, the way they look, and the way they make us feel, surely we should expect the same results from the software we use every day.

Technology alone cannot satisfy our need for more effective, more satisfying software systems. The secret of developing software that communicates clearly is the traditional process of product design that balances business and technical requirements with the needs of the men and women who use these products.

We want technology that fulfills every business and technical requirement, but our best software products also seem intuitive. This doesn't happen by accident; it represents a commitment to specify, test, and evaluate the quality of the users' experience with that product every step of the way. This is an astute business decision, because the quality of the experience a product offers will determine how well it succeeds.

It's not unreasonable to insist on business software that is easier to use, less mysterious, and far more effective—and in the chapters that follow, we'll show how to specify satisfaction.

TWO

DESIGN TO DELIGHT

Why do some everyday objects delight us while others cause us so much disappointment and even anguish?

In *The Architecture of Happiness*, Alain de Botton suggests that we feel a strong connection with some buildings because they reflect our best selves—that by expressing in stone and steel our ideals of strength, dignity, or harmony, these architectural designs touch us because they render vivid images of "who we might ideally be." What about objects that serve our everyday business needs? Perhaps no reflection of our nature could be more distorted than one projected by a typical computer system.

We've come to expect that our business software may not be easy to use—not at first, and possibly not ever. It's reasonable to expect that adopting any new technology will require an adjustment, but for most organizations, the process of implementing a new system is a major headache because it requires so much training. Almost no one wants to admit just how painful the process of adjustment can be, let alone how much it costs.

It's not considered acceptable to recognize that using new software can be such a miserable experience that it may actually lower productivity. Instead, the assumption is that extensive training is a basic requirement of any new information technology, a process that will need to be repeated as experienced workers are replaced by new workers who are unfamiliar with the system. Most managers have become resigned to the fact that no amount of training will eliminate all of the problems built into their new systems; they believe that these problems are an unavoidable result of complex technologies. The delays and errors routinely caused by clumsy software systems are accepted as a cost of doing business, and the frustration and complaints of the men and women who use these systems are ignored.

Why do so many of us have so much trouble using even the most common software products such as word processing programs? Is it because these systems are too intricate to be understood by ordinary men and women?

More than 150 years ago, Hans Christian Andersen made some observations about public perception in a tale he called "The Emperor's New Clothes," the story of a proud ruler who was so bedazzled by two merchants' extravagant promises that he became unwilling to trust his own eyes. Believing the merchants' claim that their garments were so magnificent that they could not be seen by anyone who was unqualified to appreciate them, the emperor ultimately paraded naked through the streets as throngs of his subjects stood along the road, obediently expressing admiration for the emperor's "new clothes."

Some parallels exist with the claims made for enterprise resource planning (ERP) systems, the software programs that promise to seamlessly integrate an organization's multiple business applications into one robust system that will streamline operations, reduce costs, and improve revenues, using powerful technology that will be simple to install and easy to implement. More often, the result resembles The Emperor's New Enterprise System.

The Emperor's new Enterprise System

Once upon a time there lived a chief executive officer who ruled a global empire. As much as he enjoyed fine clothes and vintage wines and traveling to distant parts of his kingdom in his Gulfstream, he was exceedingly fond of new technology. He took great pleasure in the voluminous reports produced by his corporate computers, and he ordered sophisticated software for every department of his empire. This increasingly complex network generated ever-multiplying, ever-widening streams of data.

The vast resources at his disposal attracted many vendors and consultants, and one day two strangers requested a meeting. They let it be known that they represented a renowned supplier who could provide the most magnificent information technology imaginable—an enterprise resource planning system that would integrate all of the empire's operations. Not only would this ERP system be unimaginably fast and efficient, but it also would be custom-designed. In addition, this proprietary system could not be used by anyone who was stupid or otherwise incompetent.

This would be the ultimate information technology, thought the CEO, *and it would enable me to instantly identify those who are unfit for their jobs*. He asked accounting to cut an enormous check as a down payment, and commanded the consultants to begin work.

The two consultants departed. For a long time, nothing was heard from them.

I'd like to know how the new system is coming along, the CEO thought. But when he remembered that those who were unfit for their positions would be unable to use the new system, he felt slightly uneasy, and it occurred to him that it might be better to delegate someone to investigate.

I'll send my chief financial officer, the CEO decided. *He has decades of experience, and no one is more trustworthy*.

So the CFO paid a visit to the consultants, who greeted him effusively and led him to a desktop monitor. As he watched, they swiftly clicked onto one page view after another, some filled with text, others crowded with graphs or charts, and others featuring lively animation. The poor old CFO stared as hard as he dared.

Good grief! he thought. *I can't make heads or tails of this*. He wondered, *Am I getting too old for this job? I must never let on that I don't understand.*

"Don't hesitate to tell us what you think," said one of the consultants.

"Why, this is amazing!" The chief financial officer peered at the screen through his reading glasses. "I'll let the CEO know how delighted I am." And so he did.

Soon the CEO sent a junior vice president to form her own opinion on how the work was progressing, and the same thing happened: As hard as she tried, she couldn't understand the system.

I'm sure everyone else will know how to use this, she thought to herself, *but I just don't have the technical background. I mustn't let anyone find out how stupid I am*. So she reported to the CEO, "It's everything we could wish it to be."

Word of the ERP system had spread throughout the empire, and soon everyone was anticipating its arrival with a mixture of optimism and dread, hoping it would make their jobs easier but worrying about whether they would have trouble learning to use it.

At last it was ready to be previewed. Attended by the chief technology officer, along with the chief financial officer and the young vice president who had met with the consultants earlier, the CEO was led to a seat before a large monitor. As each file flashed by, the CEO and his entourage stared intently.

The first to speak was the chief technology officer. "Extraordinary!" he exclaimed. "A triumph of technology!" The young VP and the old CFO, each assuming that the others could follow the demonstration, chimed in: "Such clever icons!" "Such vivid colors!"

What's this? thought the CEO. *It's so confusing! How can this be happening, to me of all people?* He thought hard. And then he said to the consultants, "Most impressive. My congratulations!"

And so it was that the CEO's new enterprise system was approved.

Soon the new system was installed and a splendid deployment ceremony was arranged in the conference center, with several hundred vice presidents, managers, supervisors, their assistants, and even clerks seated before monitors.

With his chief technology officer at his side, the CEO rose to his feet to praise each feature of the new system. As everyone tried to follow along on the screens before them, the CEO spoke long and passionately, until at last he concluded his remarks.

For a moment there was silence. Then the chief technology officer began to applaud, and slowly others followed, until everyone in the room was politely applauding. The CEO was all smiles. But when the applause died away, a young clerk who had been hired just that morning raised her hand.

"I don't understand how to use this system," she said. "I can't figure out how to make it work."

Then someone else said, "I don't understand, either!" And yet another said, "And neither do I." And throughout the room, others thought to themselves, *And neither do I.*

The CEO shivered, for by now he suspected that his new enterprise system was profoundly flawed. But he thought, *This system has been developed at great expense, and it has been installed, and now everyone will just have to learn how to use it.* So he held his head high as he brought the ceremony to a conclusion and strode confidently back to his office, his retinue trailing behind him.

SOFTWARE'S MISSING FEATURE

Recently I visited Washington, D.C., to meet with eight members of a large law firm whose clients include several of the world's largest software companies, and they told me about the trouble that so many government agencies are experiencing in implementing their clients' new enterprise systems. At one agency after another, managers were reporting significant disruptions and delays as their staffs struggled to learn new terminology, new passwords, and all the new procedures that the systems require.

It was clear to the lawyers that these systems were difficult to use. But although they had made an observation that was entirely accurate, they all believed that their perception was unacceptable. Despite widespread reports that the men and women who were using these new systems were learning slowly and even complaining that they hated to use them, the lawyers, like most other observers, attributed this general dissatisfaction to the human condition: *This is what happens whenever people encounter something new—especially new technology.*

Despite their professional expertise in challenging assumptions, the lawyers had accepted the problem of user adoption as a given. In this case, their skepticism had deserted them. It hadn't occurred to them to raise an objection.

Try to imagine approving a large check for any other business product that is difficult to use. Whether the price is $50 million or $50,000, we usually expect to be satisfied with a business product. We expect it to be delivered on time, and we expect it to be fully operational on the day it's delivered. Not so with the products of information technology.

Since the late 1990s, private industries, government agencies, and large nonprofits have spent billions of dollars deploying, maintaining, and upgrading enterprise resource planning systems that promised to transform the speed and accuracy of their operations. SAP, Oracle, Microsoft, and other manufacturers claim that with their wares, information will be better organized, systems and departments will communicate more effectively with one another, supplies and inventory will be managed more efficiently, and customers will enjoy unparalleled quality of service. Employees have been trained and retrained, upgrades have been installed, and expensive consultants have repaired, reinstalled, and reconfigured these systems. And still something's not right: These systems aren't working as promised. While manufacturers celebrate the transformations that they are bringing to industry, and as information technology departments point to launches and installations as successes, employees throughout their organizations struggle minute by minute with ineffective systems.

There's no doubt that ERP systems represent remarkable technological advances and a deep knowledge of many of the most esoteric aspects of business and management philosophy. Until very recently, every large organization built systems of information technology piece by piece, department by department, stringing them together haphazardly. The fact that we now have the capability to coordinate the operations of a global organization and serve the business needs of its 50,000 employees by means of a single database is nearly incredible. Yet these multimillion-dollar products are profoundly lacking in the characteristics of our most useful everyday tools: simplicity, consistency, flexibility, and responsiveness. Many of these systems are unusable.

Think of an ERP system deployed by a typical business as just another tool of the trade. Like any business tool, an ERP system is meant to be used by employees to perform specific tasks that drive the business. The relevance of the tool to the tasks of the employees and to their business should be self-evident; after all, the responsibility of the users (the employees) is to serve the business. But self-evidence is not a characteristic of the vast majority of ERP systems, and despite billions of dollars spent on intricate and typically ineffective training, employees are often forced to shift their focus from the subtleties of accomplishing a business task to the complexities of using the business tool.

Widespread concerns about the performance of ERP systems were confirmed by a study published by Forrester Research in 2003. In "App User Interfaces Still Need Work," Forrester reported that its researchers had viewed demos of ERP systems from 11 vendors, including SAP, Oracle, and Lawson, to measure how easily users could complete three basic tasks, including changing their security profiles. Forrester reported that many of the systems fell far short on overall usability, and several required "inordinate patience and expertise." The authors asked, "Would anyone buy a Porsche if shifting gears required weeks of model-specific training and a lot of muscle? Just as shifting is basic in a sports car, so are these application-management tasks." Today, too many systems still lack a basic feature—a design that makes them easy to use.

WHO'S THE CUSTOMER?

One day not long ago I was chatting with a senior sales rep for one of the world's largest software companies, and he proudly told me that his company's research was showing real improvement in customer service. After I congratulated him, I said, "How about user research—how are you doing with the people who use your products?" He paused and then said, "You've got me there."

One odd aspect of business software is that the people who buy these products are usually not the people who use them. The buyers are the chief technology officers, financial officers, directors of government agencies, and other decision makers who sign the purchase orders and licensing agreements. These executives may have broad and deep knowledge of their operations, but they lack the hands-on knowledge possessed by the mortgage processors, call-center clerks, air-traffic controllers, insurance brokers, firefighters, purchasing officers, medical records personnel, and other professionals whose daily tasks the software is meant to support. However, the software industry regards the *buyers* as its customers.

People who drive cars are called drivers; people who use telephones are known as callers; and people who read are called readers. Just as the publishing industry considers their customers to include booksellers, libraries, and readers, most industries make no distinction between those who buy their products and those who use them. Only two major industries, one of which is illegal, refer to their ultimate customers as *users*. In any context, it's an unattractive word, and its connotation of powerlessness and self-victimization denigrates the people it describes and implies that nothing of value could be learned from their experiences.

Those who buy business software and those who operate it usually have divergent viewpoints and goals, so they often have different standards in judging the effectiveness of these products. To an executive who has conscientiously labored to assemble a complete inventory of all the capabilities that software must deliver, the product succeeds if it meets every business requirement and fulfills every function on the list of specifications. To a chief technology officer, success may be to achieve the deployment of a powerful new product from SAP or Oracle throughout the organization. When the CTO flips a switch to turn it on and announces to the board of directors that everything is in order—glossing over the arduous process of training and other messy details—rarely does anyone in the boardroom have the expertise to delve beneath the surface to examine discrepancies between the software's performance capabilities and its ease of use. Yet to the workers who can't see how to use these expensive, highly touted systems, the disparity between what these products can do and how they actually work is as puzzling as extravagant praise for the emperor's mythical new clothes.

Ask the heads of five or six global corporations whether they're satisfied with their enterprise systems, and you may be told that in general, everything is fine, or even that the system is performing beautifully. More often than not, the experience of these executives in getting a complex system in place has been so time-consuming, so expensive, and so stressful that they think it's miraculous just to get the system running, and they regard any other aspects of implementation as insignificant. But if you poll a thousand employees of those companies to ask about their experiences with those enterprise systems (or, better yet, if you observe some of them at work), you may get different data.

The people who use software or any other product can easily tell you how well it works. But they may not be able to fully explain why, because a great product is more than a matter of technical wizardry or graceful styling; it's the result of good design.

In the automobile industry, design is the process that molds specifications for the driver's seat into a form that accommodates the contours of our bodies and dictates that all the controls be located within easy reach. In the practice of architecture, design is the process that creates construction specifications for buildings that please our eyes and lift our spirits, whether they be massive cathedrals of commerce that serve multiple functions or private residences with graceful floor plans that harmonize with the daily rhythms of their residents. In information technology, design is a collaborative process that links business and technology by identifying both the business needs and the human requirements, communicating those requirements to technologists, and translating technology's solutions into products that can be quickly adopted by the individuals who use them.

The traditional design process is the only method that consistently achieves practical technological solutions to complex business problems. Information technology is a powerful tool, but many of the software products we use are awkward because they've been developed without a process of design that creates clear channels of communication between technology and its customers.

In order to make software that communicates more clearly, we must listen much more closely to the men and women who use it. What we can learn from them will help us design solutions to some of our most expensive business problems.

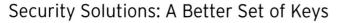

Security Solutions: A Better Set of Keys

The difference between a product that gives a business what it wants and one that satisfies its needs may be simply a matter of communication.

One of the things we want is security. We make it a priority to safeguard our proprietary business information, our financial information, our e-mail, and information about our customers. The business requirement is clear: *Protect this information from unauthorized use*. To fulfill this requirement, the software industry has amassed a formidable arsenal of defenses, including encryption software, antivirus software, antispyware software, filtering tools, firewalls, and password systems, as well as software that coordinates all these preventive measures by means of unified threat-management systems. But these technological solutions don't always give us what we need.

To provide what is needed, it's necessary to assess the human requirements as carefully as the business and technical requirements, and to identify areas where they conflict. For example, the business requirement of a security system is to lock out intruders, but the human requirement is to provide easy access by authorized users. How can a software program be secure if it's easy to open? These two conditions aren't mutually exclusive, but if they're to coexist, they must be balanced.

A security system is only as strong as its weakest link, and many of the most heavily fortified security systems are compromised because the keys are in plain sight. Most of us routinely use multiple personal identification numbers and passwords. From a technical standpoint, the more complex the password, the better. The ideal password looks like a line of code: a string of letters, numbers, and symbols, a combination that's impractical for most people to memorize even if they're willing to try. If forced to use an obscure alphanumeric code just to open the software program they need in order to do their jobs, most people will respond by keeping that pesky password handy—for example, by writing it on a Post-it and taping it to a desktop monitor.

People are much more likely to keep their passwords private if they're given the authority to choose them, so one solution is to enable people to create their own passwords. But this resolution leads directly to another conflict, because many of the passwords that people would like to use represent a security specialist's worst nightmare. From the human perspective, an ideal password is one that's easy to remember—a name, a phone number, an address, a birthday, or even the word *password*.

To prevent people from choosing weak passwords, technologists devise lists of rules. Many software products contain password instructions that look like this:

Create a password using from seven to nine characters, including:
- A digit.
- A character.
- A symbol or a special character.

- No word found in the dictionary.
- No proper name.
- No repeat of any character.
- No consecutive digits or characters.
- No punctuation or spaces.

These instructions are perfectly clear—to some people. But others will wonder, *What's a character? Does "No repeat of any character" mean that I can't use the letter "e" more than once?*

How many minutes will it take the average person to solve this puzzle? How long will most people try before they give up and phone a help line for technical support or ask to use a buddy's password?

What people need is clear information. By testing and measuring how successfully people are using a system, it's easy to identify areas of confusion and to specify solutions.

Often the solution is a simple matter of expression. Technical requirements can be expressed much more clearly by translating them into plain English and by providing examples.

Set Your Password

Choose from seven to nine letters, numbers, and symbols, including:

- At least one letter.
- At least one number.
- At least one symbol (Examples: ~ @ # $ % ^ & * + − < > =).

But:

- Don't double any letter, number, or symbol (Examples: ee 33 $$).
- Don't use any word that can be found in the dictionary.
- Don't use any proper name (the name of a person or a place).
- Don't use punctuation (Examples: ! , . ; : " ([} ? /).
- Don't use spaces.

(i) Tip: Think of a phrase to describe yourself, a favorite activity, or a goal, and abbreviate it with letters, numbers, and symbols.

Example:

• "I ride my bike five miles every Saturday" (Irmb5m@S)

These instructions fulfill the technical requirements, and by making it easier for people to follow the rules, they also support the human requirements. This equilibrium provides the security system that business wants, and it also gives business what it needs—a secure, self-service process that minimizes the number of calls to the help desk.

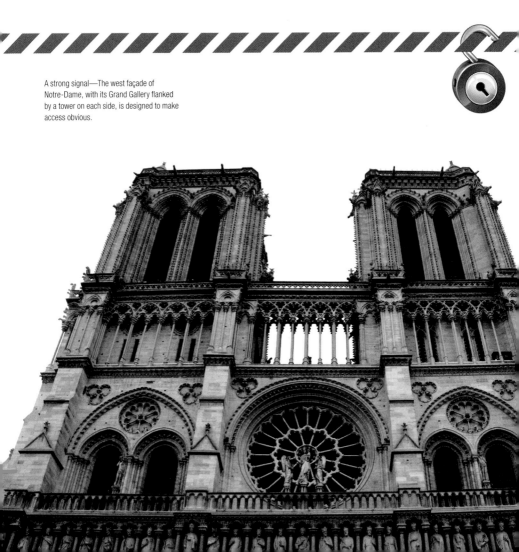

A strong signal—The west façade of Notre-Dame, with its Grand Gallery flanked by a tower on each side, is designed to make access obvious.

NAVIGATING NOTRE DAME

Design is a process that enables a product to clearly reveal its purpose. Good products are designed to be self-evident, and using them is as easy as finding your way around a well-designed building.

When you approach the Cathedral of Notre Dame in Paris, or St. Peter's Basilica in Rome, or any other great cathedral, you can identify the entrance long before you reach the first marble step. Once inside these sacred spaces, no matter how large or how intricately detailed their interiors may be, you can easily orient yourself even in dim light, and when it's time to go, you know which way to turn.

Centuries of thoughtful designs have produced thousands upon thousands of individual churches built according to the same basic plan, like variations on a theme: each one unique, but configured in ways so similar to the others that even on your first visit you feel that you're in familiar surroundings.

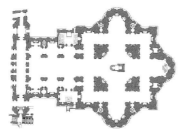

The vast cathedral of St. Peter's has a floor plan that can be immediately understood.

The same sense of familiarity is built into most of the products we use every day. If I were to hand you the keys to my new convertible, would you know how to start the car and drive it away? To answer that question, do you need to ask about the make of the car, or do you expect that the location of the accelerator and the brakes will be obvious? Once we've learned how to drive, we assume that we'll be able to slide behind the wheel of any car and take it for a spin, because the function and location of every basic feature is pretty standard. This standardization is no accident.

Automobile manufacturers long ago realized that everyone would benefit if the features of these machines were designed to be self-evident to men, women, and teenagers possessing vastly differing degrees of experience, physical dexterity, and intelligence. Although automobile styling and mechanical capabilities vary among brands, you'll also find that nearly every feature that you touch, from the handle on the door to the emergency brake, has a logical function and a predictable location. If only this were true of software products.

If you speak with corporate technology officers about the importance of design to business technology, they're likely to think of style or fashion—the contours of their laptops, the color palettes of their web sites, the shapes of the icons, and the layers of code beyond the screen—rather than the historic role that design has played in so many successful businesses.

Good design is often both fashionable and stylish, but design has different objectives. Fashion and style are what make some of us prefer a Harley and others a Vespa, but design determines which ones are easiest to maneuver. Fashion and style influence the purchase of a pair of brand-name sunglasses, but whether they fit comfortably will be determined by their design. Your favorite pair of cuff links may be vintage Art Nouveau, Art Deco, or a classic Modernist style, and they probably will be just as fashionable tomorrow as they are today, but you'd probably be much less fond of them if their shanks were so poorly designed that you had to fiddle with them each time you wanted to lock them in place on your sleeves.

Design has a job to do. Although design creates products that may be beautiful to behold, its greatest value is in the successful execution of its responsibilities, whether it's a soaring architectural silhouette that symbolizes our highest ideals or the screen of an automated teller machine that shows how to make a withdrawal in a matter of seconds.

COMMUNICATING BY DESIGN

All designers are communicators. They may be trained in graphic design, industrial design, interior design, architecture, or fashion, but all designers are commercial artists who devote themselves to the practicalities of form and function. Through collaboration with one another and with specialists in many other professions, they create most of the things we use every day.

Fashion designers apply their knowledge of human physiology and psychology, their appreciation for social and cultural contexts, and their understanding of materials and manufacturing techniques to create clothes that serve a function and provide a sense of delight. Wearing something that fits comfortably and looks great is a satisfying experience, whether it's something as sensible as a pair of sneakers with Velcro closures, as playful as a Swatch watch, or as elegant as an Hermès scarf that envelops its wearer in a sense of luxury. These products are successful not only because of how they make us look, but also because of how they make us feel.

Graphic designers communicate by means of visual messages. The international symbols for "Men" and "Women" are the work of graphic designers, as are the traffic signs that caution us to expect a sharp curve in the road just ahead. Graphic designers who specialize in wayfinding, mapping, and environmental design work closely with architects to create directional signs and symbols for corporate campuses, retailers, hospitals, theme parks, universities, and cities. Although we may barely notice these pictograms once they have been posted along hallways and freeways, they enable us to maneuver through the airport in Frankfurt to locate our connecting flight as easily as when we are in Kansas City.

Graphic designers also create the distinctive logos that become the familiar faces of international brands, and they originate legible type-faces for computer screens and telephone books. They collaborate with psychologists, engineers, and computer programmers to design animation for corporate training programs and video games, and they create realistic 3-D simulations that can showcase condominiums that are yet to be built, demonstrate precisely how to perform surgical pro-cedures, and monitor the movements of space satellites.

Many graphic designers work in the traditional disciplines of print and television advertising, magazine and book publishing, and films; some specialize in creating exhibits for trade shows, visitors' centers, or museums. In every medium to which they apply their expertise, graphic designers are storytellers. Whether their assignment is to create educational touch-screen displays for the National Constitution Center or to develop an intranet for a global banking institution, the mission of every graphic designer is to communicate a clear message that attracts and holds the attention of its intended audience.

Just as graphic designers use visual media to communicate, indus-trial designers communicate through form. Like graphic design, the practice of industrial design has utilitarian objectives, yet many of its products are as stylish and as appealing as any creation of fashion. Most of our favorite objects are the products of industrial design, a relatively young profession that emerged in the first half of the twentieth century in response to rapid development of mass-production techniques for making consumer products and the availability of new materials.

Through collaboration with engineers and manufacturers, as well as with corporate managers and marketing specialists, industrial designers create products for the automotive, communications, and consumer electronics industries, as well as every other sector of business. In the 1930s, industrial designers worked with aero-nautical and electrical engineers to produce such marvels as DC-3 commercial airliners, inexpensive Bakelite radios, and television sets with 12-inch screens. Polaroid cameras and colorful, light-weight fiberglass chairs were introduced during the 1940s, and the 1950s became a golden age of automobile design with the release of Ford's 1955 Thunderbird, Volkswagen's 1956 Karmann Ghia, and Chevrolet's 1957 Bel Air.

Sketches by Jacques Gréber enabled citizens of Philadelphia in 1917 to imagine the great future of the Benjamin Franklin Parkway. These drawings helped to refine the plan and build consensus.

Many industrial designers now specialize in electronic consumer products such as digital cameras, cell phones, and minicomputers, all of which are developed with the use of computer-assisted design programs that are themselves the products of industrial design. Without industrial designers there would be no Eames chairs and no Rabbit corkscrew, but industrial designers also create water purification systems and scientific instruments, and those who specialize in ecodesign strive to balance consumer needs with the conservation of resources and energy by developing innovative products such as low-flush toilets, hybrid cars, and furniture made from renewable materials such as bamboo.

Furniture, housewares, and other familiar products of industrial design also may be created by architects or by interior designers, who plan the furnishings and decor of so many of our public and private habitats. Interior designers can soothe our senses with sumptuous furnishings in subtle hues or fire our imaginations with a dramatic mix of pattern and color. They can transform an industrial warehouse into a conference center, and they can make a pediatrician's waiting room seem as welcoming as a playroom. In each case the responsibility of the designer is to learn from the client as much as possible about how a space is meant to be used in order to modify the interior to serve those activities.

Architects, environmental designers, and urban planners specialize in organizing space. Working in three dimensions, they conceive plans for the places where we live, work, worship, and educate our children. Their specialties may be as broad as city planning or as specific as a singular residence with furnishings and fittings customized right down to the doorknobs.

Architects may practice industrial design, graphic design, interior design, civic design, landscape design, engineering design, or electrical design, and they may have expertise in historical preservation, industrial parks, luxury condominiums, bridges, shopping malls, wineries, power plants, or sports stadiums. Equally important as the job of developing a set of blueprints for a project is the architect's responsibility to act as liaison between the client and the project's engineers, contractors, and suppliers. In addition to writing specifications, developing and monitoring schedules, and managing the process of construction, architects often prepare environmental studies and assist with applications for zoning permits.

In order to fulfill their role, architects must understand the complexities of their clients' needs as thoroughly as they understand the properties of steel and titanium. Our greatest works of architecture enhance the activities that take place there and make it possible for us to comfortably move within those spaces. Just as theaters and concert halls are environments designed to promote entertainment and creative expression, a well-designed corporate headquarters building has an exterior form that expresses its purpose, its importance, and its spirit, while its interior spaces facilitate the work that is done there. Architects recognize that our work is an important part of our day. They know that the environment in which we perform our tasks has everything to do with how effective we are, and that our work environment even helps to define who we are, as employees and as employers.

For the headquarters of Johnson Wax in Racine, Wisconsin, Frank Lloyd Wright gave its main office an open, spacious floor plan with nearly half an acre of unobstructed space, and in place of conventional windows he installed layers of glass tubing to flood the workspace with soft, indirect light. Since its completion in 1939, this building has exemplified workplaces that nourish the human spirit.

Workplaces that lift our spirit lighten our load. Tools that are easy to operate, directions that are clear, and furniture and clothing whose

forms fit the shapes of our bodies satisfy us because they have been created by a collaborative process of design that considers our needs. This traditional process of design has been consistently used to develop residential and commercial buildings, highway systems and subway maps, dishwashers and kitchen utensils, BlackBerrys and iPods, and every major category of business and consumer products except one.

In the race to deploy new information technology, businesses and software developers often have stumbled because they have ignored traditional methods of product development and have seriously miscalculated the risks of developing software without pausing to find out more about how this new technology will be used. The information technology industry, still in its adolescence, has been in too much of a rush to stop and tie its shoelaces.

Brand experience begins at home. These workspaces reflect organizations that consider how a workplace affects its workers. Energy, innovation, and excitement characterize Frank Lloyd Wright's "Great Workroom" at the Johnson Wax head-quarters in Racine, WI (top) and the global offices of Bloomberg L.P., as illustrated in its New York City headquarters.

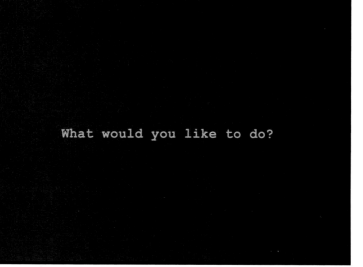

What would you like to do?

Teaching Etiquette to an ATM

In my first job after college, I was lucky enough see what can happen when a global business insists that its software be designed to meet the requirements and the expectations of its customers.

During the 1980s, executives of Citibank began to refine the company's fleet of automated teller machines—not to improve the technology of the machines, but to improve the experience of using them. In order to make the ATMs more appealing to their customers, they were working on a plan to deploy touch-screen technology. They knew that this new technology would work, but they recognized that its success hinged on making appropriate and maximum use of all the advantages that this new hardware afforded them. They also knew that adding touch screens would not be enough.

Citibank knew that unless its customers wanted to use the ATMs, they wouldn't. The bank's leadership recognized that if their ATMs were to provide the competitive advantage they were seeking, they would have to offer customers an experience as comfortable and as satisfying as having tellers provide personal assistance with deposits and withdrawals. In fact, in order to gain widespread acceptance, these ATMs would have to offer something far more important than 24-hour access to cash: They would have to be easy to use.

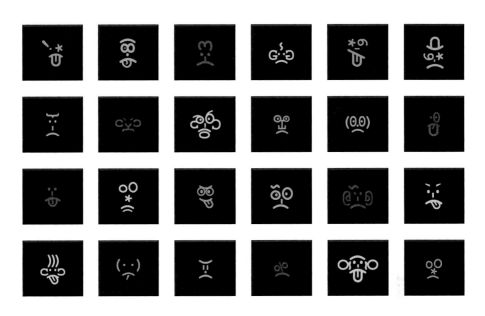

The company had an immense stake in persuading more of its retail customers to adopt automated teller technology. The opportunities for increased revenues and savings were enormous, but the cost of developing and implementing this new technology was much too large an investment to undertake without utilizing every reasonable precaution to minimize the risk that too few customers would use it.

Citibank had long realized that cash machines represented a challenge of design as much as technology, and in 1989 the bank had hired a large design firm, Two Twelve Associates, to provide consulting services. This firm had designed street signs for Manhattan and wayfinding systems for Disney World, and designing wayfinding systems to be used inside computers was a natural extension of that work.

That spring I had graduated from Carnegie Mellon University and had begun a job as a freelance designer with Two Twelve Associates at its offices in New York City. Initially, the firm assigned me to work with Citibank on a new program to help the bank's customer-service representatives market the bank's products. But by the end of the year the economy had slowed, and one day I came back from lunch and found out that the project I was working on had been mothballed. Instead, I was told, I'd be working on cash machines.

Citibank had already completed a rollout to markets in New York, San Francisco, and Washington, D.C., and the bank was working on prototypes for Germany, China, and the Middle East. These ATMs were created

exclusively for Citibank customers, and they were somewhat different from ones we see today. They were installed in kiosks, and each one was located in an enclosed foyer that complemented the decor of the branch's main lobby, right down to the red velvet rope that showed where to form a line. After hours, these mini-lobbies could be entered only by swiping a Citibank card through a slot, so the kiosks were private and secure. Other banks were just plunking down big terminals at the corners of their buildings, but Citibank had been carefully thinking through the experience of using these machines and was approaching it from the viewpoint of its customers.

Other project teams had already designed the features that enabled customers to withdraw cash and make deposits. My job was to design and prototype more advanced transactions such as applying for a new account, transferring money, and purchasing a certificate of deposit. Our process was to analyze each task and break it down into a series of steps, figure out what the most logical sequence of steps should be, and design screens to accomplish each of those steps. Every screen contained a few words of instruction that customers touched to register their choices.

Crafting the words for the very simple displays on these screens was a huge challenge. In order to do this, I was not working with a programmer; I was sitting beside a linguist who was choosing the words one by one. We knew that we had to put as few words on those screens as possible, so every word mattered. Each word had to present information accurately, in nontechnical language, but it also had to convey an appropriate tone. One of our innovations was to replace the standard series of commands with a first-person voice. For example, rather than the blunt directive, "Select One: Deposit, Withdraw, Transfer, Purchase a CD," our screen began by asking, "What would you like to do?"

Once we created the scenarios that we imagined would work on the screen, we'd send them to the lab for testing. To my utter delight, the lab was located in the Daily News building, the 37-story Art Deco landmark at 220 East 42nd Street. The building is best known for its dramatic,

```
Select a Transaction
   10/02/88    Deposit       250.00        ↑
   10/05/88    Withdraw       50.00
   10/05/88    Withdraw       50.00
   10/05/88    CHK #0019     267.05
   10/06/88    Withdraw       40.00
   10/09/88    Deposit      1146.08        ↓

                                            OK
```

domed lobby, whose centerpiece is a gigantic rotating globe. To a kid like me, just out of college, being there was like working in the headquarters of the Daily Planet. The lab was located in the basement, but it was a beautiful test environment; it looked like the lobby of a bank. Four cash machines were lined up, and volunteers were given a set of instructions to read and a list of tasks to perform. Citibank recruited volunteers by enclosing a solicitation in its monthly statements offering its customers a cash fee of $50 to participate in a 45-minute test. The response was excellent, and Citibank received a steady stream of volunteers representing every imaginable sector of its business.

As we observed the volunteers, we not only measured their ability to complete a transaction successfully, but we also evaluated the quality of their experience. In an observation room, monitors provided us with images captured from multiple cameras trained on each volunteer, as well as an audio recording and an image of what each volunteer saw on the screen. All of this data gave us insights into what every volunteer was doing, and why. After each volunteer had completed the test we asked, "What do you think about what you did? How did you feel about it?"

Once our tests confirmed that customers could easily use one feature, we'd move on to the next. But we quickly learned that the form of expression most appropriate for New York would not necessarily work everywhere else. When the screen text was translated into German and tested, word came back that the informal, first-person script that had

been welcomed by the New York market was far less successful in Germany. These customers, we discovered, felt uncomfortable about having a banking machine speaking in this voice. They strongly preferred more direct language, and Citibank was sensitive enough to recognize that and modify the language accordingly.

At every step of this process we were all asking ourselves, "How can we make people feel comfortable about using a computer to access their bank accounts?" The solution could not be found in technology. But we knew that with the right design, we could effectively communicate with nearly every individual and appeal to them on several levels, not only by enabling them to complete a specific task, but by helping them to feel good about it.

Despite my good intentions, I was often humbled to see how far off the mark my designs could be. One feature we tested was designed to enable customers to review a history of their checking accounts, to see which checks had cleared and to look at other transactions. The screen could display only five items at a time, so I said, "Here's what we'll do. We'll put scroll bars on the left and right sides, and people can scroll through the data, five items at a time." I thought it was a no-brainer: Let's get it done and let's get it down to the lab. So we got it down to the lab and we tested it—and no one could figure out how to use it. In 1990, almost no one knew how to scroll. In my little world, I knew about scrolling, so I'd assumed that everyone else knew, too. The solution was simple: one button to *Page Up* and another to *Page Down.* People were accustomed to seeing pages; that was the form in which their statements were sent to them.

The happy ending to this extensive process of designing, testing, redesigning, and retesting was that Citibank achieved an exponentially greater level of user adoption for its cash machines than any other bank. The project set a standard for designing software that fulfills business needs as successfully as it serves the men and women who use it, but it became a magnificent exception to the way in which most software is developed.

THE HUMAN FACTOR

Designers who specialize in information begin by finding out how a product will be used.

The first question is *What does this thing need to do?* Its job might be to reorganize a data storage system, expand an intranet portal, or provide a program for customer-relationship management (CRM). The next question is *Who will use this product?* What sort of experience and technical abilities do these individuals possess? Do they speak a common language? Why do they need this product? How will their environment affect the way they use it? Will it be used by investment counselors seated at their desks, or will it be used by emergency-room physicians?

Answering these questions means gathering information from many sources. To define and prioritize the goals of a project and to identify its business requirements calls for teamwork among designers and an organization's chief information officer, business analysts, product managers, and other executives. To learn what tasks the product must perform—its functional requirements— it's necessary to examine business processes and workflows. Understanding the needs of the people who will use the product requires expertise by those who understand the human mind and the human hand—specialists in the science of human factors.

Cognitive psychologists, behavioral psychologists, and other experts in human factors bring unique value to the software design process. They're trained observers whose knowledge of the human mind and body enables them to recognize patterns of thought and behavior, and they can draw upon new research in psychology and physiology to test products and prototypes. They may conduct research through surveys, by observation, and by posing pointed questions: *Is there anything confusing about this product? What obstacles does it place in your path? Is it consistent? Does it make you feel confident? Does it permit you to gracefully recover from errors?*

Specialists in human factors also can measure performance: What percentage of a group can successfully complete a specific task using this product? How long does it take? What is the rate of error? Knowing the answers to these questions before technical specifications are finalized will have a dramatic impact on the success and the ultimate cost of the finished product.

To give form to both the business requirements and the human requirements, designers and human factors specialists collaborate with the builders—the software analysts, engineers, programmers, technical writers, and other technologists who perform the meticulous work of construction.

This process is most effective when designers, human factors experts, and technologists work side by side with users to test early versions of a product by evaluating progressively detailed sketches, schematics, and prototypes.

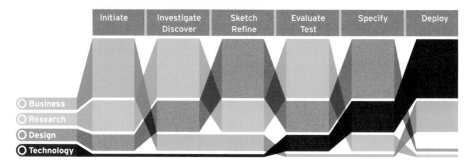

| Initiate | Investigate Discover | Sketch Refine | Evaluate Test | Specify | Deploy |

Business
Research
Design
Technology

A successful process of design includes multiple disciplines at every step, allowing each skill to lead at certain points. Early concepts are influenced by technology, but not restricted by it. Later, technical implementation is checked for its faithfulness to initial strategies and goals.

When these specialists work as a team throughout the development process, they produce practical products in a suitable form. The right form might be a dynamic 3-D graphic, or it might be a process so inconspicuous as to be almost imperceptible, but in each case the answer to a problem begins with a series of questions.

Designers contribute expertise derived from numerous disciplines; they may be trained in graphic design, industrial design, architecture, or urban design, or in the newer disciplines of information architecture, interaction design, or environmental design. Yet all designers share the same goal: to create products that respond to human needs.

FORM, FUNCTION, AND SPIRIT

Until recently, if you drove on a toll road anywhere in the world, you would have to stop the car at some point to pay the fee. At best, this would result in a short delay and the momentary inconvenience of lowering the window and fumbling for change, currency, or a credit card. At other times, it would mean an excruciating wait in a long line.

Beginning in the 1980s, technology offered drivers an alternative, as wireless devices with names like E-ZPass, FasTrak, PikePass, E-Pass, I-Pass, and PlatePass began to appear on the front windshields of cars throughout the United States. These electronic tags, each one programmed with an identification code unique to its owner, respond to radio signals beamed from toll booths, and within a few seconds after a car enters the "read zone," a device in the toll booth can decipher a car's code, transmit a request for authorization from the driver's account, confirm approval, and flash a green light to let the car zip by.

The technology for these devices, radio frequency identification (RFID), had been used as early as World War II to identify planes as friend or foe, and bar codes based on closely related technology had been in commercial use since the 1960s. But although the major technical problems had long ago been solved, the electronic toll-collection devices were innovative because of the way they were designed to be used.

As soon as technologists had figured out the mechanics of the computerized communications and accounting systems, their work was essentially done. From a technical standpoint, the device that is attached to the windshield would function just as well if it were manufactured in the form of a handheld gizmo that you could hold up as you approach a toll booth and store in the glove box the rest of the time. It might have become something as small and slender as a card that you could carry in your wallet. Either version would have been an effective technical solution to the business problem of automatic toll collection, and even could have improved traffic flow. But the final form—a hands-free device that needs to be touched only twice, at the beginning and end of its useful life—is not only more efficient, but it's also incomparably more appealing because it gives us a sense of freedom.

Products that are well designed have value beyond necessity: The defining feature of a great product isn't its power, its size, its speed, or its novelty. We value things according to the quality of the

The sketch at left is an early prototype of Frank Lloyd Wright's design for the Guggenheim Museum—a low risk test of his concept. Below, the finished design as it exists today in New York City.

experience we have when we use them. The physical form of a tool matters greatly, but even a form that satisfies a product's functional requirements may not come close to meeting our needs. A great product doesn't just do its job; it does something more.

A hundred years ago, American architect Louis Sullivan popularized the design principle that "form follows function," and he practiced his philosophy by using new materials and technologies to design buildings whose inventive forms reflected their purposes and their interior structures. But Sullivan also integrated into the exterior designs of his office buildings elegant ornamentation that complemented and balanced the geometrical outlines of the masonry walls with flowing terra-cotta vines and other organic shapes inspired by nature. Even today, the logical configurations and graceful details that he designed for Chicago's Auditorium Building and for the Wainwright Building in St. Louis engage our minds and refresh our spirits.

Long after Sullivan's maxim had become widely known, Frank Lloyd Wright, who once had been his chief draftsman, maintained that Sullivan's philosophy had been misunderstood and his words given too narrow an interpretation. "Form and function," said Wright, "should be one, joined in a spiritual union."

THREE

SPECIFY INNOVATION

Software for wireless computers, digital notebooks, and other tools of information technology puts vast amounts of data at our fingertips, but often the information we need remains just out of reach.

STRANDED AT HEATHROW

Flashback: I'm sitting in the lobby of the Hilton Hotel at Heathrow International Airport with the sales director from my London office as we finalize a proposal for a new client. The client is one of Europe's largest banks, and this will be the largest contract my technology company has ever signed, so for us this is pretty exciting stuff.

Are we sweating access to a wireless network? Not at all; we've come to this hotel because we know it will work. Are we worried about the details of the deal? No, we've been through this hundreds of times before; we know how to do this. There's a problem, though:

The word processor on my colleague's laptop just won't correctly format our last edit.

Our client wants a graphic that describes the project we're proposing, and he wants it as soon as possible. I offer to help. I paste the graphic into the document and drag it into position. The screen freezes. A display announces, "Not Responding." I quit Word. I re-open the file. I start over and immediately begin saving my changes. The screen freezes again: "Not Responding." I'm optimistic. I reopen the application, then the file. Before long I'm frozen out again. I re-create the file from scratch. Once again it freezes.

I can't figure out how to make it work, and I have a deal waiting to be signed. My sales director is paid on commission, so this is as important to him as it is to me.

"*How the hell do you. . . ?*" Our exchange grows more and more tense as we try to format the document. We've worked for a year to build a relationship with this bank, and this contract will be an important strategic win for us. Now, after countless e-mails, meetings, discussions, and trans-Atlantic flights, suddenly a poorly designed tool is standing between us and success. We estimate that between the two of us, we've been using Microsoft Word for 20 years. And here we are—with this thing blocking the communication between two pretty smart professionals and their client.

Man vs. machine in 1936: We know how Chaplin felt.

I feel like Charlie Chaplin in *Modern Times*, trapped in the cogs of an unforgiving machine. Although I'm in no risk of physical harm, the risk is real and considerable because I'm at the mercy of a machine whose creators haven't taken the time to make it easy for me to operate this so-called productivity tool.

DON'T BLAME TECHNOLOGY

From the earliest days of the Industrial Revolution, the relationship of human beings to machines has been difficult to equalize. Our history of conflict with the machines we build to serve us isn't surprising, because our respective capabilities and limitations are so different. When we successfully manage these differences, they become complementary sources of strength, but when we fail to fully acknowledge and accommodate them, they cause so much friction that they can bring the simplest task to a standstill.

The Industrial Revolution set in motion massive machines that were designed with little regard for their operators, many of whom were children.

Computers are fast, accurate, and consistent, and they excel at repetition. They can respond instantly to the correct cues, but they have no sense of time; their prodigious memories have no sense of history. They can't be distracted by anything around them, and they're not affected by a mood or a commute. They're rigid, but they can be modified. Most of the time, they do exactly as they're told.

The behavior and thought processes of human beings are variable, flexible, and unpredictable. Our memories are subject to error. We receive information through our five senses, none of which is fully understood, and we interpret that information according to our individual experience. We can recognize complex patterns. We're highly sensitive to our environment, and our emotions influence our actions. We're creative thinkers who can solve problems in surprising ways. We have goals and expectations. We take risks.

When we use a machine that responds to our needs, we experience an interaction that feels natural. Good software can make a task seem like a pleasure, but we routinely waste time and burn energy struggling with software that seems indifferent or even obstinate. The difference between these two experiences has nothing to do with the sophistication of the technology or the quality of information it provides, but it has everything to do with how well the software is designed to communicate with us.

Unless data is expressed and displayed in a form that can be understood by human beings, it's inaccessible. More often than not, software speaks a strange dialect. Despite the detailed specifications of the business community and their precise execution by expert technologists, most software communicates awkwardly, delivering messages that are ambiguous, incomplete, misleading, or incomprehensible. It's not unusual for a business or a government agency to spend millions of dollars on a software product to collect and reorganize vast amounts of data, only to find that the data has been stored in what amounts to a locked warehouse.

Many studies have been made of the widespread and persistent difficulties of using information software, and a few years ago I had an opportunity to take an unscientific sampling of this problem when the British Honorary Consul in Philadelphia, Oliver Franklin, asked me to host a tour of my company for a group of visitors. My guests were ten executives of a life insurance company headquartered in London, and as we sat around a conference table I described a study we had recently completed. Our client had invested more than $75 million to create a magnificent repository of data about its customer relationships, its sales, and its marketing efforts. This software, a customer-relationship management (CRM) product, had been purchased from an internationally known supplier and had been customized to the firm's specifications to give its thousands of brokers access to a myriad of data. But the brokers weren't using it. The firm had checked and rechecked to verify that the software met every technical specification and to confirm that it performed each function required of it, but still the brokers weren't using it. The firm asked my company to find out why.

When we conducted tests to observe brokers as they tried to use the software, the problems were obvious. The technology was terrific, and it had the capability to fulfill every business need, but the software required brokers to perform so many time-consuming, illogical actions that it was counterproductive. Missing from this extremely powerful product was a structure that reflected the nature and sequence of the brokers' tasks, their workflow, and the complex relationships among the multiplicities of data at their command.

As I described our findings to my visitors, I could see that the story struck a chord, so I asked if any of them had had a similar experience. One man wrote a number on the back of an envelope, saying, "This is how much we spent on that system, and we couldn't use it, either," and handed it to the woman on his right. One by one, each person sitting around the table added a number, and by the time the envelope was passed to me, the total was more than £70 million. Each of these executives had tried to implement a similar product from the same manufacturer, a company that was then an industry leader and one of the world's most respected suppliers of

CRM systems. In other words, each of these seasoned executives had invested millions of pounds in one of the best products of its kind and had nothing to show for it.

How is this possible? Despite continuing advances in technology, why do these problems persist?

It's not a lack of technical know-how or business expertise or even a shortage of time or money that accounts for software's failure to provide the information we need. The source of most of the trouble is a fundamental conflict between human beings and their machines, a conflict that causes profound misunderstandings.

THE TRANSPARENT DASHBOARD

The secret of converting buckets of data into electronic information that is easy to locate and convenient to use is simple: The messages that the data are meant to convey must be crafted by someone who respects and understands the conflicting requirements of business, technology, and the people who use the technology. Good communication requires an understanding of the audience for whom a message is intended, and this is regarded as conventional wisdom among marketing experts and media companies as well as by successful manufacturers of most consumer products.

Our cars give us very clear information from the moment we start the ignition. Under the hood, cylinders are firing and thousands of separate interactions are taking place, but a glance at the dashboard tells us what we need to know. We can see whether the oil level is adequate and whether we have enough fuel. We can see everything we need to confirm that all the systems are in order, and we can correctly evaluate them to make appropriate decisions.

Imagine checking the dashboard to view the engine temperature and seeing that it registers 121C/250F. What does this mean? You may recognize instantly that your car's engine is overheating when it registers 121° Centigrade or 250° Fahrenheit, but don't you find it convenient for the temperature to be expressed as a condition—too hot, or not? Thanks to the work of automotive designers, every bit of data on the instrument panel is communicated to us in a form that we can absorb without having to perform a calculation. A dangerously low oil level isn't expressed in fluid ounces or milliliters, a number that would require us to remember the maximum capacity of the tank and figure out the current quantity of oil relative to that capacity, but as a warning light. When we press the accelerator, the speedometer expresses our speed in terms of distance, as the number of miles or kilometers we will travel in the next hour at our current rate of speed.

Expressing data in terms of relationships, and communicating these relationships in simplified visual form, results in messages that are both clear and meaningful. Designers use the same techniques to create software for management dashboards that organize, monitor, and analyze business information from multiple sources and provide visual summaries of complex data. The best of these corporate dashboards convert data to information that identifies trends and enables viewers to react quickly.

When Green Means STOP

Every message has three parts: sender, signal, and receiver. For a message to be successfully delivered, clear language and a reliable transmitter are essential, but that's not nearly enough to guarantee that it will make sense to those who receive it.

For a message to be correctly interpreted, the signal must be attuned to the receiver as well as to the context in which it will be received. Any incompatibility between the signal and the receiver will distort the message or break the chain of communication.

Consider a stop sign: Its signal is as clear as can be, and its old-fashioned format is practical and familiar. How could it possibly be misunderstood?

But imagine a sign elegantly lettered to read *STOP*. And what if the word were positioned on a green background?

Believe it or not, last year my wife and I saw a sign just like that, posted at an intersection in an affluent suburb of North Carolina.

What were they thinking?

The makers of that sign willfully ignored the fact that for almost everyone over the age of three, the color green conveys a specific message: Green means *go*. To compound the confusion, *STOP* and **STOP** do not mean quite the same thing to most of us. *STOP* might be misinterpreted as a polite suggestion, perhaps even an invitation subject to the driver's discretion. But the message delivered by the word **STOP** is unequivocal: It's a direct order.

Whoever conceived that decorative green *STOP* sign disregarded the context, the experience, and the deeply ingrained expectations of drivers who have been conditioned to continue through an intersection at the sight of a green traffic signal. In giving no thought to how their message would be received, the makers of that sign were oblivious to its potential danger. A confusing traffic sign that creates even a momentary distraction can cause a collision that can kill.

It's possible to argue that drivers should be paying close enough attention at intersections to interpret the message correctly and react accordingly. But those who send a message without considering its context may find that they are placing those who receive the message at risk—and they do so at their own peril.

LISTENING TO THE RECEIVER

A message sent to a human being is aimed at the most complex, most variable receiver in the universe.

Whether it's delivered in the form of a traffic signal, an annual report, a printed social invitation, or an e-mail, every message will be interpreted within a context, and its effectiveness will be determined by how well it relates to the people to whom it is directed: their abilities, their knowledge, their culture, their needs, their preferences, and their physical environment. Yet many of the messages delivered by software are produced without adequate consideration of their context and without a full understanding of how they will be received.

Despite all the resources at the command of the information technology industry, its communications skills leave much to be desired, especially in comparison with old-technology companies. To minimize the risk of producing products that will be confusing or unappealing, most consumer industries make it their business to communicate directly with some of the people who use their products.

Industries as diverse as manufacturing and food service routinely use focus groups to help shape their products, and some pharmaceutical companies organize online panels for people who have a personal interest in certain diseases. Some companies take the trouble to see exactly how their products are used. To conduct a study for its shower products, Moen Incorporated recruited volunteers who agreed to videotape themselves at home as they showered. "We thought it would be hard to recruit people, but that was the easy part," said Daniel C. Buchner, vice president for innovation and design at the Massachusetts design firm Continuum, which worked with Moen on the project. "The hard part was making a camera that wouldn't fog up." The tapes showed that people closed their eyes about half the time as they showered, and that because of poor shower design they often risked injury. The information influenced the design of a new showerhead that became a best seller.

Most service industries also pay close attention to the needs and desires of their clients; specialty retailers and restaurateurs keep track of the personal preferences of their best customers, and managers of luxury hotels survey their guests to learn whether they're traveling for business or leisure and which amenities they consider most important.

Techniques like these represent rich sources of information about how consumer products and services are perceived, how they're being used, and how they might be improved. Some survey techniques are more effective than others, depending on how they're applied and the expertise of those who implement them, but they achieve their greatest potential value when they are employed early in the process of product development, when the information they offer can influence the final form of the product.

Researching the needs of people who use software is crucial. Business executives and software developers might think they know exactly how their software will be used, but they may have blind spots, and only research can confirm their hypotheses. Whether software is designed to operate a password system or to record clinical data, it's important to answer these questions:

Who will use this software? Are they members of a highly diverse group of individuals (employees of a large company, including seasonal employees) or do they have a great deal in common (emergency-room physicians)? What information do they have that will help them use this tool? What else do they need to know? What will help them understand?

What are they trying to do? What task are they trying to perform? Why do they do it? Exactly how do they do it? Do they all perform this task in the same way? How often do they repeat the process? What do they need to have to do the job more quickly and more accurately?

What's the context? Where are the people who are using this software? Are they at their desks or on their feet? What is their physical environment like? What's happening around them? Are they under time pressure? Are they trying to do anything else at the same time? How does what they're trying to do relate to other tasks? What does the workflow process look like?

What's the status quo? If the purpose of a software product is to improve efficiency, what benchmark information is available to measure present performance? How long does it take, on average, to complete a certain task? What is the average success rate? What's the rate of error? How much time do these errors cost? How are they resolved? What kind of workarounds do people use to complete the task? How long does it usually take to learn to use the current tools?

The more precisely these questions are phrased and the more accurately the answers are measured, the more valuable the information will be. You'd think that it would make sense to find out exactly how a product will be used before releasing it into the marketplace, and you'd be right. But much of our software is developed through a process that neglects to gather basic information about the people who will use it and the work that it is intended to support.

"PEOPLE ARE DIFFERENT"

Psychologists have a saying that the first scientific principle of their discipline is that people are different—in their knowledge, experience, physical aptitudes, cultural background, and personal preferences.

Even if every individual possessed the same cognitive and motor skills and the same point of view, research would be needed to answer the question of how best to phrase and format an electronic message to that person. The question becomes all the more challenging when it's considered in the context of an interactive communications system used by dozens or even thousands of individuals.

A generation ago, it became technically possible and economically feasible to delegate much of the repetitive work of human resources (HR) administrators to software that can provide answers to standard questions about policies and benefits, freeing human managers to tackle more complex tasks while giving them new tools for record keeping and recruitment. Research makes it possible to identify 80 percent of the questions that will be asked by employees in most organizations, and a corporate HR portal that automatically provides a smooth path to the information that employees most often seek—expressed in words they understand—justifies its investment many times over. But the efficiency of these electronic administrators depends on how well they communicate with their audiences.

One of the most common barriers to communication is language. Technical jargon and acronyms can obscure the simplest message, and even nonspecialized words can sabotage communications.

Imagine an 18-year-old high school graduate at the start of his first job who logs on to his company's intranet to verify his pay period: Is it twice a month or every two weeks? He's been using computers since he was five years old; he buys music from iTunes, orders socks online from Lands' End, and maintains his own blog. To find out how often he'll be paid, he opens his company's home page and locates the human resources section, where he sees several categories. He might not be able to decide whether he should click on "Benefits" or "Policies," so he might search for "pay." If that doesn't work, he might scroll through several categories of information before typing in "salary" or even "compensation." When that doesn't help, he might ask a co-worker for advice. It probably won't occur to either of them to search for the keyword commonly used in some HR software products: *remuneration*. In the meantime, their work has come to a standstill.

The time that ticks by while puzzled employees try to locate the information they need online or speak with someone at a help center represents hidden costs that can steadily drain profits. Often these expenses can be dramatically reduced without writing new code, simply by reconfiguring existing software to provide more logical navigation and a more accessible vocabulary.

Research about the people to whom a message is directed can provide answers to important questions: *Do they understand the message? Do they want this information? Are they able to use it?* But questions like these are nearly impossible to answer without observing a product in use, measuring its effectiveness, and modifying it to accommodate the needs of the people who use it.

Lowering the language barrier: automated card-sorting exercises (bottom) can identify effective words, and tests with users can yield unexpected information.

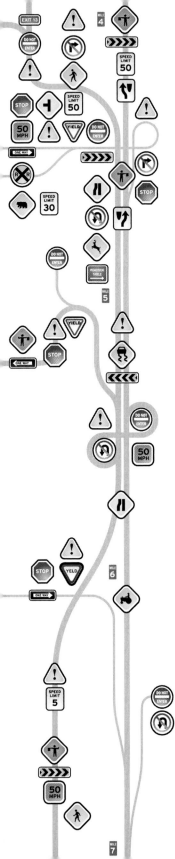

Removing Roadblocks

Technology is making it possible to give drivers much better information about traffic conditions, and new methods of collecting and transmitting data have stimulated the growth of traffic-tracking companies that can deliver up-to-the-minute information customized to the needs of individual drivers.

Several years ago one young company, Traffic.com, began offering customized traffic reports in selected cities. Drivers in Kansas City, Miami, Seattle, and more than 20 other cities could visit the company's web site to register their commutes and choose when they'd like to receive free reports on congestion and estimated delays. These reports, updated at least every five minutes, could be automatically sent to subscribers at a certain time on certain days or whenever traffic on the route became congested, or both, and the information could be delivered via e-mail, cell phone, through a car's navigation system, or as a text message beamed to a BlackBerry. The data to create the reports were compiled from wireless roadside sensors and other devices installed by state transportation agencies, toll-payment systems such as E-ZPass, information gathered from police scanners, and other sources.

Despite the technical challenges of providing continually updated information about changing traffic flow along thousands of routes, the system worked, and it offered clear benefits for individuals as well as for commercial subscribers rushing to meet just-in-time delivery deadlines.

But Traffic.com had a problem: Too few people were signing up for its service.

The procedure to register for the free service seemed easy enough; drivers needed only to log on to the company's web site and provide personal contact information and detailed information about their routes. Lists of major thoroughfares were provided for each metropolitan area so that drivers could select the names of the streets and highways they traveled, from their starting point up to the location of their destination, without having to type in each name.

The number of visitors to the site was encouraging, but the number who registered was disappointing. What was wrong? Couldn't people locate the registration page? Were they having trouble registering? Without observing people as they used the site, there was no way to know, so Traffic.com asked my company to evaluate the usability of the site.

We enlisted 14 local high school graduates between the ages of 25 and 64 to take a one-hour test. All of them commuted at least three days a week, all had basic computer skills, and eight of them already had registered with Traffic.com.

One evening, the first group of volunteers arrived at our headquarters in Philadelphia and were seated before desktop monitors in our usability lab. Each of the lab's computers is equipped with an unobtrusive digital camera, a built-in microphone, and specialized software that produces synchronized recordings of keystrokes, speech, and facial expressions. This makes it possible to track and analyze exactly how each person interacts with a software product—each false start, every pause, and any grimace of frustration.

The volunteers were asked to follow directions on the screens in front of them to register with the site, record their commutes, and perform a few other simple tasks. Next door, behind a large one-way mirror, several representatives of Traffic.com followed the progress of each participant by watching monitors linked to those in the lab.

Using the scientific method to investigate a problem requires multiple experiments to confirm the results, but sometimes just one test can point to the source of a problem. Most members of the first group of volunteers repeatedly hesitated, and it was clear that they were having trouble. A few days later, when we analyzed the tests of all the volunteers, that first impression was confirmed: Twelve of the 14 volunteers—85 percent—had failed to correctly register their commute on their first try.

The data from this three-hour experiment gave us a tremendous amount of information, and it was obvious that

the site's directions were confusing. As a first step to specify their commutes, drivers were asked, "What road do you want to start on?" After selecting a road from a list, drivers were asked, "How did you get on that road?" Some volunteers were so confused by that nonsensical question that they never progressed beyond the first step. Others didn't understand how to specify their destination or how to save the route. Even some drivers who had successfully registered their routes before volunteering for the test couldn't repeat the process.

The problem wasn't a lack of interest in the free service, and it wasn't the quality of the technology. What was needed was better communication: clear language, logical directions, an enhanced presentation of maps, simplified graphics, and a graceful navigational structure. But only a diverse group of individuals who actually tried to use the software—men and women of varying ages and abilities—could have told us this.

To test usability, a researcher guides a user in trying out a prototype as others observe through a one-way window.

EASY AS PIE: THE TALE OF A TOOL

Information from people who use a product has a benefit far beyond its potential to increase efficiency: It can stimulate innovation. Here is the story of how one person's observation of another person's needs inspired hundreds of new products.

One April evening in 1979, a small party was unfolding in the modest Manhattan apartment of a young woman named Rosemary. Among her guests was an upstairs neighbor, an attractive, 26-year-old industrial designer named Patricia Moore who had worked for renowned designer Raymond Loewy a few years earlier. During that period Moore had been collaborating on designs for the interiors of a hydrofoil and a new Russian automobile when she realized that the vehicles would be comfortable for young adults but unsuitable for older, less dexterous passengers. As she later recalled in her autobiography, *Disguised,* Moore began to wonder: How would products be different if they were designed for someone like her favorite grandfather, "Dutch"?

Reasoning that designing products for millions of senior citizens would make business sense, she persuaded Loewy to give her a leave of absence to study biometrics, the science of measuring biological information, and gerontology, the study of the biological, psychological, and sociological effects of aging. By the time she descended the stairs to join the party at Rosemary's apartment that spring evening, she was enrolled in master's degree programs in human development and psychology at Columbia University.

Uncomfortable and even dangerous, this crude tool was long considered acceptable.

As she mingled with the other guests, she began chatting with a young woman who worked for NBC's *Saturday Night Live* as a makeup artist. Suddenly Moore had an idea.

"Look at my face," she said, "and tell me if you could make me look old."

That chance meeting was the beginning of a unique research project. With the help of her new friend, who showed her how to add 60 years to her face with prosthetic jowls and theatrical makeup, Moore developed and refined a realistic disguise. Wearing a white wig, earplugs, and orthopedic shoes, her fingers wrapped with tape under her gloves and her legs stiffened by Ace bandages, she began to research how it might feel for an octogenarian to turn on a lamp, open a bottle of aspirin, use public transportation, and take part in other aspects of daily living. For the next three years she regularly conducted these experiments in Manhattan and in 115 other cities in the United States and Canada. In 1982 she put away her disguise to focus on her own design firm, utilizing her knowledge of gerontology to design products that would be easy for everyone to use.

Seven years later and more than four thousand miles away, in the South of France, Sam Farber and his wife, Betsey, were making apple pies. Farber had sold his successful cookware company, Copco, and he and Betsey were settling in for a stay in a house they had rented in Provence. Sam noticed that the arthritis in Betsey's hands was making it painful for her to peel apples. He took a close look at the vegetable peeler she was using, with its dull, rusted blade and its hard, skinny handle, and he began to wonder why it was made the way it was. From a manufacturer's standpoint it was perfect: a cheap tool that was easy to produce and

Big idea—The OXO peeler was shaped by an understanding of human needs.

one that would quickly need to be replaced. He realized that nearly every utensil in their kitchen was uncomfortable to use.

Sam Farber knew kitchenware. His uncle Simon had founded Farberware cookware in 1900, and Sam had worked for his father's company, Sheffield Silver, a maker of trays and servers, before he founded Copco in 1960. He began to think about going back into business.

When he and Betsey returned to the United States, Farber got in touch with a New York City industrial design firm, Smart Design, which had done work for Copco, and began describing his idea. He wanted to develop a new line of high-performance kitchen utensils that would feel comfortable, especially for those with limited strength, movement, or coordination in their hands. Smart Design employed designers who specialized in ergonomics and social science, but for this project they wanted even more specific expertise, so they called in a consulting design firm.

By this time Patricia Moore's company was prospering. Her specialty of designing easy-to-use products had attracted major clients such as AT&T, Johnson & Johnson, and Kimberly-Clark, and she had consulted with 3M, Procter & Gamble, and Merck Sharp & Dohme to develop more convenient packaging for cereal, laundry detergent, and medicine bottles. To Smart Design, her firm looked like a natural fit to collaborate on its new project.

Working together, the two design firms created 21 practical, good-looking, dishwasher-safe kitchen utensils, including a bottle opener, a can opener, a grater, a ladle, a spatula, a pair of kitchen scissors, and a vegetable peeler. They gave the vegetable peeler a stainless steel blade and a fat, rounded handle shaped to rest comfortably in the hand and made from a soft, rubbery synthetic that wouldn't become slippery when wet. The handle also had a generous hole that made it convenient to hang near the countertop.

Sam Farber called these new gadgets the Good Grips collection, and to market them he formed a company called OXO, a name he chose because it can be read from any direction.

When Farber introduced Good Grips at a San Francisco gourmet show in April 1990, he was confident that his new utensils would succeed because they met a need.

"I have never come up with a more meaningful product," he later said. "Everything you do all day puts pressure on you: opening refrigerator doors, range doors, closets. The environment has failed to meet our needs, so we must rehabilitate it. These are products for people, and good products always sell. The profits come after that."

That month Sam Farber wrote orders for $750,000, a clear sign that his innovative idea, stimulated by his wife's personal need for a little more comfort and convenience, had broad appeal. The company grew rapidly, and in 2004, after several changes of ownership, OXO was purchased for $273 million by another American consumer products company, Helen of Troy Ltd. Today OXO produces more than 500 kitchen, garden, and automotive tools, and its vegetable peeler can be found in the collection of the Museum of Modern Art as well as in the kitchens of millions of people around the world.

Easy to see—
This OXO cup has measurements printed inside, so there's no need to lift it until it's filled.

WHAT WE NEED TO KNOW

Where does innovation come from?

Innovation is the difference between asking what needs to be done and asking how it might be done better. If you were to ask someone to explain to you how to peel an apple, you might conclude that nothing more would be needed to get the job done than a sharp piece of metal. And technically, that's true. But if you had witnessed Betsey Farber's discomfort as she tried to manipulate a dull, clumsy tool, you could have seen other possibilities.

Unless we take the trouble to investigate the ways in which people use a product, we may replicate its limitations and miss information that would suggest opportunities for innovation. When we observe and study the context in which a product is used, we often find out things that we didn't expect. Innovation may be something we don't know we need and don't know we want until we see it.

Innovative software is driven by partnerships between business, technology, and design in a collaboration that considers the specific ways in which the technology will be used. To produce better software products, we need to provide a clear interpretation of the data that is available to us. To interpret data appropriately, we need to understand the context in which it will be presented. To correctly evaluate its context, we must understand the people who will use the software, and this can be accomplished only by doing research to discover their aptitudes and their needs.

My struggle with word processing software at the hotel near Heathrow was memorable not because my predicament was unusual but because it was so unnecessary. The task that we were trying to accomplish was simple, and after a few more minutes of intense effort, we were able to wrestle the material we needed into alignment. The finished document was accepted and signed, and

A new form—In 1951, Chicago physician Edith Farnsworth wanted a weekend home, and architect Mies van der Rohe took the opportunity to challenge the standard specs.

it became the beginning of a successful partnership with our new client. But the painful memory of using that blunt tool endures.

Our present technology offers us a wealth of capabilities to communicate with each other, to conduct our business, to educate, and to entertain. Software gives physicians better, faster ways to analyze diagnostic information, throws open the doors of the greatest museums and libraries of the world, and enables geologists and ecologists to gain a better understanding of the earth's natural resources, from the oil fields of Alaska to beyond the Great Barrier Reef. But all the data in the world won't tell us what we need to know unless it's presented in a form we can use.

The opportunities for innovation that we can achieve through information technology are almost beyond imagining. But if these innovations are to be meaningful, they must be informed by the everyday needs of those of us who use them.

FOUR

CONSIDER THE CONSEQUENCES

Many executives reason that their employees can learn to operate almost any business system, given the right training, and that if technologists can deliver sophisticated electronic tools that automate routine tasks, the least people can do is to put up with a few quirks in the way the software performs. Some employers expect workers to recognize that it's in their best interest to adapt to whatever challenges their tools present to them: After all, what choice do they have?

According to this philosophy, most of the problems that people have with software can be explained in terms of a learning curve, and as workers become more familiar with the software they use, their proficiency will improve. When this doesn't happen— when significant numbers of workers have trouble using a business system, and familiarity breeds only frustration, resentment, and hostility—the common assumption is that more training is needed. All too often, the result is low productivity and an endless cycle of training as experienced workers are replaced by new hires.

It's true that some people manage to adapt surprisingly well to even the most counterintuitive software, and it's not unusual for some to become experts in navigating the maze on their desktops. But asking people to use inferior tools, or placing the right tools in the wrong hands, can have unintended consequences.

LESSONS FROM THE UNDERGROUND

As a subway car approaches London's Baker Street station and slows to a stop, the doors slide open and a recorded voice warns, "Mind the gap"—reminding passengers to watch their step as they cross the space between the threshold of the car and the platform. It's a small thing, but it's emblematic of the ways in which allowances need to be made for the gap between the mechanics of technology and the needs of human beings. Many years ago, in seeking to meet those human needs, the London Underground developed an innovative tool that has influenced transportation systems around the world.

The London Underground was regarded as a marvel of engineering in 1863, when a three-mile stretch of track was completed to make it the world's first underground railway. As steam locomotives were replaced by electrically powered trains, the Tube's network branched into a dozen lines serving 255 stations along 250 miles of track. This busy transportation system, which is used to make three million journeys each day, would be a bewildering labyrinth of interconnected caverns if not for one thing: It has a brilliant map.

The present map of the London Underground was designed more than 75 years ago by a draftsman named Harry Beck. Until 1933, the map of the London Underground looked like a road map. Its wiggly lines faithfully depicted the twists and curves of every route, and these meandering pathways were overlaid with detailed information about the streets, communities, and landmarks above-ground. For map users, sorting out all this data was a challenge, and Beck realized that what passengers most needed was information to help them relate their location to their destination: *Is*

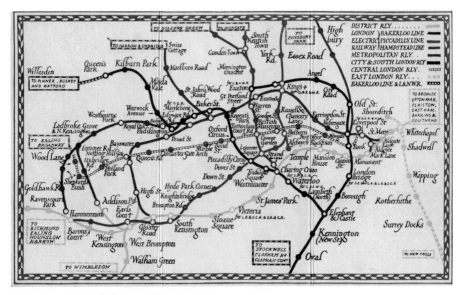

Early transit maps of the London Underground displayed geographic
data that was of little use and made the maps too complex.

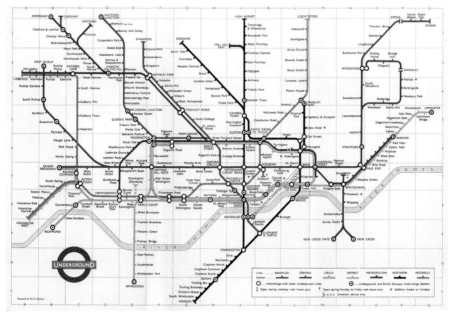

Just what we need—Harry Beck knew that the best subway map
would accurately reflect a thorough understanding of the system and
an accurate understanding of the user's needs, and would anticipate
the information travelers want.

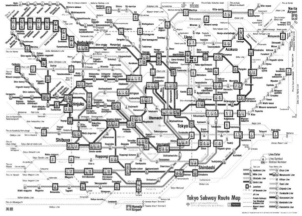

A 1933 map
has influenced
many modern
subway maps
from Washington,
D.C., (left) to
Tokyo (right).

Washington D.C.
map courtesy of
© WMATA.

Paddington the next stop, or the one after? Beck radically simplified the map by depicting the routes as a series of intersecting straight lines in bright primary colors, giving each route a different color. As the Tube continued to expand, Beck's map was updated, but its basic design remains unchanged and has become the inspiration for maps of other rail and bus systems from Tokyo to Washington, D.C.

If you were to ask people what information they want from a subway map, they'd probably tell you that they want the map to show them how to get from one place to another and that they also want the map to show them where they are at all times. If you were to accept those two requirements at face value and convert them to specifications, the result probably would be a literal interpretation, a document as overloaded with information as the confusing maps produced before 1933. But Beck understood that what people want isn't necessarily the same thing as what they need. His skill as a designer and his personal experience as a passenger enabled him to present the required information in a new form, a clear diagram that can be easily grasped—a map that speaks of sequence rather than distance, relative position rather than exact location. By interpreting what was wanted, Beck was able to provide what was needed. In doing this, he created a most useful and usable user interface to a complex and potentially confusing system.

The Workaround Wizard

When we find ourselves facing a barrier that seems insurmountable, we look for ways to work around it. When software raises an obstacle, business executives, lawyers, physicians, and other professionals often work around the problem by delegating the task. Those who can't delegate must find other alternatives.

Not long ago I visited a large call center in the Midwest where I had an opportunity to see a stunning workaround solution. The call center is a sales office operated by a telephone company that employs several hundred people to sell the company's services, using a telemarketing script pushed to operators via a proprietary software product. The company was dissatisfied with recent sales, and management wondered if the software needed to be updated, so my company was asked to evaluate the system.

As a first step we arranged a visit by a designer and a cognitive psychologist who would observe the work processes, and because this was a major new client, I joined them, representing the design team. As our host led a tour through the call center, he explained that the sales agents were using software that had been customized to meet very specific business requirements.

To find out how the system worked, I asked my host to introduce me to the center's best salesperson, and he led me down a hallway to a cubicle occupied by a pleasant middle-aged woman. I pulled up a chair beside her desktop monitor and asked her to show me how she used the software to make a sale. One by one, she patiently demonstrated every feature and showed how to navigate around the error messages that routinely appeared on the screen. As she explained, I silently tried to anticipate each step, but the process seemed insanely complicated, and many of my guesses were wrong. Her understanding of the idiosyncrasies of the system and her ability to manipulate this unwieldy sales tool were impressive. Throughout this tutorial she continued to wear the headset that she used to speak with customers while a display board overhead blinked and beeped insistently, announcing a steady flow of incoming calls, yet not once did she interrupt herself to take a call. Her calm demeanor and lack of urgency suggested that she was accustomed to ignoring callers in order to focus on the software. Not once during her explanation did she mention sales, and it was obvious that she wasn't thinking about sales because the job of managing the software demanded her full attention.

After thanking her, I excused myself and rejoined the manager who was hosting our visit.

"I'd just like to confirm something," I said. "Is that your best salesperson? Does she sell more than anyone else here?"

"Not really," he said. "But she knows the system better than anyone else, and that makes her incredibly valuable. Everyone goes to her when they have a problem."

"But this is a sales office," I reminded him. "The most valuable people are the ones who sell the most, right?"

"You could look at it that way," he agreed, "but if I didn't have her, who would people ask? No one else understands how to use the system as well as she does."

I realized that the most highly valued sales agent in the office was essentially a superintendent who knew how to keep the facilities running. She wasn't a star when it came to sales, but her patience, her experience, and her attention to detail had gradually enabled her to become the expert who helped everyone else figure out how to circumvent all the obstacles they confronted in using the company's software. She had become the Workaround Wizard.

I bit my tongue while I tried to think of a more diplomatic way to tell my host, "Well, I'd like to please speak with the people here who know how to move product and who are hitting their numbers so that we can discover how this tool works for them and what part of it is good for them and what part of it gets in their way and prevents them from doing their job of selling."

All around the Workaround Wizard sat men and women who probably had the potential to become outstanding sales agents but who were stuck with a tool that almost no one knew how to use. They were so preoccupied with mastering the status quo that it seemed unlikely that any of them were thinking about new ways of using the software to improve sales. What a strange business dynamic: The company had come to value employees more for their ability to manipulate an inferior tool than for their impact upon the business.

At most call centers turnover is high; the average tenure may be as short as 16 weeks, with as many as four weeks devoted to training. Business software that's easy to use lowers the cost of training and raises productivity. Sales agents who can do their jobs without assistance feel less stress and provide better customer service than agents who need to put their prospects on hold and interrupt their co-workers to ask for help.

Software that's intuitive promotes innovation by creating opportunities to think creatively about new ways of gathering, organizing, and using information. But when the act of using software is a struggle, most people simply leave it to someone else to rise to the challenge, master the system, and become the Workaround Wizard.

CONTINUOUS EDUCATION

Some idealists believe that all software should be so easy to use that there would be no need for manuals or training sessions. That's a realistic goal for software that runs an ATM, a search engine, or a web site. However, we accept that it takes training and practice to learn how to drive a car and to operate most other complex machines, so even though manufacturers may claim that their software is easy to use, it's reasonable to expect that some training will be needed. The question is, *How much training—and how often?* More importantly, *What is actually being trained, and what will it cost?*

Training represents a major portion of the cost of implementing most business software.

As a rule of thumb, the process of implementation usually costs at least as much as building or buying the software—sometimes twice as much. One U.S. consulting firm, Accounting Software

Advisor (ASA), has estimated that if you plan to purchase $25,000 worth of accounting software, you also should expect to spend an additional $25,000 to $50,000 to implement it, depending on whether your office is located in Birmingham, Alabama, or New York City. ASA calculated that training typically represents nearly 30 percent of the cost of implementation. Add to this the recurring cost of training to keep pace with attrition, and training expenses become even more significant. For software with a price tag of seven figures or more, the training costs can be staggering.

Because buyers have an enormous stake in acquiring business software that minimizes the cost of training, ease of use often heads the list of business requirements. Software manufacturers acknowledge this demand by promoting the "user-centered design" of their wares, offering "safe passage" to business solutions "at the speed of business" with software that's "transparent" and "people-ready." If only it were that simple.

Everyone wants software to meet the needs of the people who use it, but who are those people, and what do they need? Specifying software that's easy to use is like ordering a car that's fun to drive. Are you thinking of a nimble two-seater that hugs the road or a four-wheel-drive vehicle that can transport you and your family and all your camping gear up a mountain trail? Whether business software will be easy to use depends on how well it's matched with the people who use it and the environment where they operate it.

If you believe the advertising campaigns for business software, you'd never expect that learning to use these systems could be a problem. Some ads for brand-name software portray the companies that use their products as comfortable enclaves populated by a contented workforce. Misleading advertising is nothing new, but I challenge you to find people who have as much genuine enthusiasm for the software they use in their workplaces as they have for the power tools they use in their home workshops or the professional-grade gas ranges they install in their kitchens. Try to imagine hearing someone say, "I love this portal that was just installed on my desktop! This thing rocks!" It just doesn't happen, but it so easily *could* happen.

It's entirely possible to give people software that enables them to do their jobs more quickly, to become better informed, and to make better decisions—things they would really like, because these things would allow them to feel more confident and to work more effectively. It wouldn't even cost as much as paying them to learn to use ineffective tools.

Most people have a great capacity to solve problems and to learn from them, but the more counterintuitive the software, the longer it takes to learn it. Those of us who routinely use even the most basic software have come to assume that when the word "Start" appears on a computer screen, it also may mean "Stop"—that much has quickly become obvious, as illogical as it seems. Most people can learn to remember when it's necessary to take a step backward or sideways in order to take the next step forward, and it's also possible to teach employees that information about their paychecks and other forms of compensation can be found by searching their corporate intranet for the word *remuneration*. But it takes time to learn to use software that seems confusing or poorly organized, and during this time many undocumented delays and errors occur as people work their way through the process and think to themselves, "Okay, I made that mistake once; I made that mistake twice; I made that mistake three times, and I'm not going to do that again." And they don't. So eventually, perhaps weeks or even months later, people may be able to operate the system efficiently. But why would any organization want to make a continuing investment in teaching people to use inferior tools?

Like the Ford Motor Company nearly a hundred years ago, today's software manufacturers expect their customers to make a significant effort just to operate their products. But unlike Ford, which provided a free tool kit in each car, manufacturers of major software products charge to provide the expertise needed to operate their products, and these tools may cost twice as much as the product itself.

At a recent professional seminar, the chief information officer of a regional health system approached me and began to describe the "successful" experience he was currently having with the deployment of a system he had purchased for his hospital. Smiling, he proudly told me that in order to ease users into the new system, the vendor had installed "trainers" on every floor of the hospital, 24 hours a day, for the first weeks of the system's launch. "They'll answer questions and remind people of the things they learned in training—get them used to the system," he said. Ford provided tools—not a person in the backseat! Without considering anything else, the idea of adding this many human beings to the hospital floor, notwithstanding the attendant risk of introducing additional germs, gave me pause.

At its present stage of development, the software industry has more in common with the swimming pool industry than it does with the automobile industry. Once the product is installed, it's expensive to reconfigure, but it offers the supplier a steady stream of revenue in the form of maintenance fees. The competitive race to bring products to market adds another incentive for software manufacturers to deliver upgrades and new bundles of features as quickly as possible and to consider the human consequences later. In this way, training has become a profit center rather than a tool designed to advance business goals.

A few years ago my company was consulting with a brokerage that was preparing to deploy new customer-relationship management (CRM) software for its large database. The firm had scheduled extensive training for each of its brokers and all their assistants— four hours a week for eight weeks. My first question was, "At the end of this training, are they going to be better brokers, or are you just teaching them how to use the tool?" The response was very quick: "Oh, they're just learning to use the tool."

It seemed to me that from a business standpoint, this should have been totally unacceptable. Shouldn't training be an exercise in

Lowering the learning curve—To check how well a data-entry tool will fit the context of its intended use, this sketch from a designer's note pad records information about how caregivers interact with each other and transmit information.

teaching new ideas and concepts that will improve performance? What is implied with most systems training is that *If these people learn to use this software, they will be better at their jobs.* But it's not necessarily so. Many systems as they present themselves to end users are so unfamiliar and unpredictable that they limit the number of safe assumptions individuals can make about the tool based on their own experiences within the organization. When system design doesn't consider even basic characteristics of the user's experience, training must become a program focused solely on the tool. Very often, training programs concentrate on teaching people to *un*learn much of what they know about the business. Rather than teaching everyone how to perform familiar tasks in illogical ways with a difficult tool, the goal of those 32 hours of training should have been to show how to use these new tools to maximize business by communicating more effectively with clients. But in the process of mastering the complexities of the tool, its purpose had been forgotten.

If the people who use these products are the source of the problem— if most of us are just too stupid to see how to use these magnificent new wonders of technology—then there's little that businesses can do to avoid making continuous investments in training. But if the problem is caused by a failure of communication between the partnership of business and technology and their intended audience, there's a better solution.

BUILDING ON ASSUMPTIONS

Many of the problems that encumber software can be prevented by practicing a method of development that is dedicated to researching the requirements of business and technology together with the needs of the users. This is the process that guides the construction of our homes and offices.

Architects who specialize in commercial buildings are expected to organize the interior and exterior spaces of their buildings in logical ways and to observe other conventions that will enhance the tenants' experience of occupying these spaces, and long before they begin to write specifications they meet with their clients to define their needs and learn about their preferences. The process of designing a residential building is more personal, but whether a building is commercial or residential, an architect is responsible for gathering very specific information about the client's wants and needs, and designing physical forms that satisfy these needs. To accomplish this, architects make copious drawings to illustrate and document the plans, validate the plans through systematic review by the client, and collaborate with engineers to provide the contractor, the suppliers, and all the craftspeople who execute the project with precise specifications and blueprints that leave nothing to the imagination.

The best business software is built through a collaborative process that parallels the architectural process, both in its methods and in its division of responsibilities. The most effective development teams include not only the client (stakeholders and subject-matter experts from the business side) and the builder (software developers), but also designers who can interpret, balance, and communicate to technologists the business requirements as well as the needs of the people who will use the product. The designer's job is to find out what the client wants, to identify what the client genuinely needs, and to design the physical form of the product—and in doing so, to also design the experience of using it. Accomplishing this requires close communication among business, design, and technology, with visual prototypes and frequent reviews.

In a perfect world, during the design phase of software development the client will be shown prototypes for evaluation and testing at regular intervals so that adjustments can be made to match the technical performance of the software to the work processes of the company and the needs of the people who use it. In the real world, deadline pressures compress the review process, and despite the best intentions of stakeholders, life gets in the way. Travel schedules, sales conferences, and other priorities intervene. Even worse, the development process may be organized in a way that excludes some of the people who need to be at the table. Most software is developed without designers or their methods, by business analysts and programmers who inappropriately assume the role and responsibilities of designers. Those most likely to be left out of the process of developing software are the people who know how to design it and those who will use it.

If you were to hire an architect to design a new residence or to renovate your existing home, you'd expect that the two of you would have a great many conversations. The architect would ask what functions the structure will need to serve: *Who will live here? Are there any children? How many bedrooms and baths will you need? How many cars do you have? Will you want a gym? How much storage space do you need? Do you have any pets?*

Your architect also would want to know how you and your family plan to use your home: *Do you like to have an informal breakfast with your children, in a room where it's okay to spill things? Do you keep many documents in your home office? How do you like to entertain? Could you use two dishwashers? Will you want guest accommodations in a separate wing?*

In addition, your architect would ask about your goals for the house: *Should the plans allow for expansion? What kinds of energy efficiencies would you like to achieve?* And of course you'd be asked what architectural vocabulary seems most natural and most appealing to you: Georgian? Postmodern? Mediterranean?

After gathering all this information, your architect would begin making sketches on paper to show how your house might look and how each room would physically relate to the others. Once you'd reached a consensus on the approach, the design would be developed, from concept drawings to 3-D models. During the planning process you'd be shown diagrams of progressive complexity, reconfirming each feature. If you have no experience in reading schematic drawings, your architect probably would make additional drawings to explain how various elevations will look, and later you might be shown computer-generated images of each room.

Throughout the design development phase, you and your architect would collaborate in making decisions about the features that would be built into your house and the ways you plan to use them, and your architect would interpret these decisions through specifications that would reflect engineering considerations such as the structure and location of the plumbing, electrical, and security

systems. At each stage, you'd be shown working drawings and samples of materials to be sure that everyone agrees upon how the finished result should look: *The library will have built-in bookshelves and lateral file drawers, and this is how they'll look; the deck will be made of recycled teak, and here is a sample that shows the grain of the wood and its color.*

Once you'd given your approval, your architect would express these decisions as blueprints and specifications and would oversee their execution by the general contractor, the builders, the electricians, and the plumbers. The specifications could spell out the construction and components of your house down to the last doorknob: the pitch of the roof, the width of the hallways, the location of the security alarms, and thousands of features inside the walls that you'd never see. Throughout the construction phase, you'd be able to visit the site, monitor the progress of the project, and test each feature.

The most effective business software products—those that anticipate and satisfy our needs—are developed in a way that parallels this process, starting with an analysis of how the product will be used. But although some information architects and software designers have both the communications and design expertise to gather and interpret this information, the great majority of individuals assuming design responsibility are technologists who do not possess those people skills, and business analysts who are simply not qualified to design a product.

Too often, software is "designed" by professionals who have little information about the users of their products and no experience in prioritizing their needs or designing ways to satisfy them. The result is widespread confusion among those who use business software and intense frustration among the executives who approve its purchase. Well-informed buyers of business software who know exactly what they want nevertheless often find themselves unable to acquire the tools they need, and even executives who enjoy the luxury of being able to customize or build proprietary systems for their organizations commonly discover that a big budget and exacting business specifications won't necessarily produce a product that people will use.

Assuming that a technologist can successfully select or build the software that is needed—without enlisting the help of someone who has the communications and design skills of an architect—works about as well as asking an engineer to build a house.

If you were to contract with an engineer to build your house, both the process and the result would differ substantially from your experience with an architect. The process probably would begin the same way. In your initial meeting, you'd be asked many questions to define the size, the style, and the functions of the house and to specify its features. Your engineer would leave with pages of information, and soon you'd probably receive a copy of the notes summarizing that meeting in the form of a tidy bulleted list: a two-story residence with four bedrooms and en suite bathrooms; two half baths; a kitchen and breakfast room; a living room; a dining room; a library; a gym; a deck; a two-car garage. Once you approved the inventory of basic features and the budget, you'd be given a schedule for completion. No problem, right? *Wrong!*

The next step might come many months later with a message notifying you that your house is finished—that it's been built to code, and all the mechanicals have passed inspection. Everything works perfectly. Now it's time for you to take a walk-through to learn how to operate the heating and cooling systems, the lighting systems, and the security system.

You'd probably be surprised by what you'd see. Suppose that your two young daughters have each been given a bedroom on the second floor, but they like to share a room, and neither of their bedrooms is large enough for two. Imagine that the dining room seats 12 comfortably, but you often host dinner parties for 20. What if no one had asked whether you have pets, and you'd been given a security system with motion detectors and a kitchen floor with an ebonized finish that shows every speck of dirt tracked in by your three dogs? Picture stepping onto a spacious deck that has no place to plug in an electric grill.

Of course, all this can be fixed. You can add an outlet on the deck, refinish the kitchen floor, modify the security system, cut a hole in one wall of the dining room to expand it, and build an extra bedroom on stilts off the second floor. In the meantime, you could

make do: Run an extension cord from the kitchen to the deck by threading it out a window, disarm the security system, ask your daughters to squeeze into a tight space, and expand your dinner parties into the living room by setting up card tables. It would be awkward, but you could manage. In fact, you might decide that the inconvenience and expense of shutting down the kitchen to refinish the floor isn't justified, and it makes more sense to just live with it and tolerate the necessity for constant maintenance. You might not even notice hundreds of smaller defects.

Many companies struggle with software that doesn't come close to meeting their needs because of small deficiencies and major misunderstandings caused by guesswork—problems that could have been prevented by asking more questions, analyzing the answers, and questioning assumptions.

SPRINTING TOWARD SECOND-RATE

A product is only as good as its specifications.

Business analysts and engineers have the knowledge and skills to develop software that's both functionally complete and structurally sound. But neither a technologist nor a business analyst is a skilled designer. Just as architectural engineers can join lengths of steel to span a river or bend sheets of glass and titanium to form a curvaceous shell for a concert hall, software engineers can build almost anything, but the more they know about how the finished product will be used, the better it can be. Simply having a business analyst describe the optimal set of features and functions is an incomplete charter. Technologists need to know more in order to build an information architecture that's practical, comfortable, and appropriate for the people who will inhabit it for hours at a stretch.

As with so many other ventures, the ultimate success of a software development project is often determined at the outset. Unless the requirements document for a new information system contains the same sort of detail that architects elicit from their clients about how people will use the system and how they will navigate within it, the best efforts of brilliant technologists may result in a compilation of functions and features that are inconvenient or even unworkable.

During its short history, the software industry has utilized a variety of approaches to develop its products. Like most professionals, computing technologists have invented their own jargon to distinguish themselves from other practitioners and to brand their activities and their products. They call their products "applications" or "systems" and they refer to portions of those products as "deliverables." The software industry has given its development processes active, muscular names inspired by nature and sports—waterfall, agile, rapid, sprint, scrum, spiral, and even extreme programming. Microsoft and many other companies call their development process the Software Development Life Cycle (SDLC). The distinctions among these methods, and their relative merits, are energetically debated by professionals, but the most significant differences among them are essentially a matter of how the work is organized: *How many phases of construction will there be? How often will progress be verified?*

Any production process can be envisioned as a cascading progression of many small steps, and a generation ago one of the most popular approaches to software development was the waterfall method. Developers who use this method attempt to document all the requirements at the outset and then work through successive phases of specification and coding before proceeding to test the product and release it. The inherent flaw in the waterfall method is that the farther a project progresses and the more massive it becomes, the more difficult it becomes to shift its course in response to changing business requirements and to control the nature of its terminus.

Newer, more flexible approaches such as extreme programming, rapid, and agile divide projects into segments that can be completed in short bursts of activity, with deadlines as frequent as every two weeks or every 30 days. In these methods the approach is to identify each task, write the code, test the code, and deliver that unit; repeat the process with the next unit; then test both units together and deliver; and so on, until the project is complete. Essentially, this is nothing more than a series of small—extremely small—waterfalls.

All of these methods have more in common with one another than they do with classic processes of product design, a development process in which the human requirements are as important as the business and technical requirements. Most products are designed, tested, and built according to specifications that identify the needs and the habits of their potential customers, and the success of these products can be measured by the response of the people who use them.

The fact that many of our software products communicate so poorly, and the reason that they seem so socially awkward, may be a legacy from the early days of computing technology, when computers communicated primarily with one another under the watchful eyes of highly trained humans. Software built to interact exclusively with other software has clear requirements, and the development process can be largely automated; specifications to fulfill the business and technical requirements can be generated by software, the code can be written by software, and the code can be tested at each stage of the development process by other software. Technically, this method is highly reliable, but it doesn't work nearly as well in producing software that must respond to human interaction, such as software that helps human resources professionals manage compensation and benefits, recruit and schedule personnel, and make performance evaluations, while allowing employees to fill out a W-4 form, locate information about holiday schedules, and update their emergency contact information. Human resources software is a flourishing specialty, and at prices ranging from $5,000 to more than $250,000 you can choose from a variety of products that promise to fulfill your needs. But no matter how closely the business requirements have been specified, your satisfaction with these products will depend on how well they satisfy the human requirements.

One of the most persistent myths in the industry is that if business specialists can define a problem, technologists can deliver the solution. This might seem logical in light of the software industry's astonishing technical capabilities, and the standard processes of software development are based on this presumption.

If a business needs something as simple as a sales report that will be updated more frequently, the functional requirements can be

WATERFALL METHODOLOGY

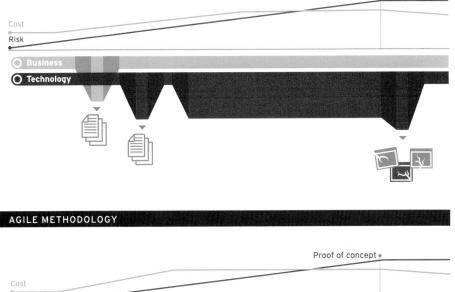

AGILE METHODOLOGY

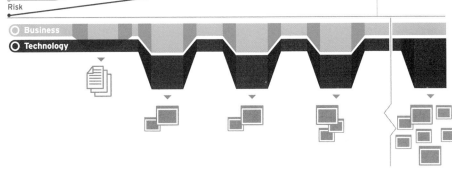

PRODUCT DEVELOPMENT

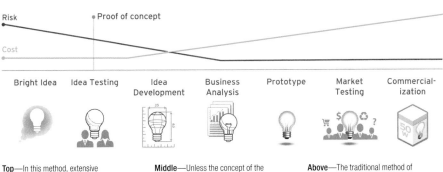

Top—In this method, extensive documentation is followed by a long, costly, programmer-driven process that allows risk to peak at a very late stage.

Middle—Unless the concept of the software is proven at an early stage, a comprehensive view of the product isn't visible until risk has peaked, even when code is delivered in short bursts.

Above—The traditional method of product development keeps costs low until a product has been tested and risk has been minimized.

easily expressed: *This is the information the report must contain, and this is how often it must be updated; this is how the information will be entered, and this is how it will be saved.* Once the functional requirements have been defined, the technical requirements can be specified: *This is the software that's needed to organize the sales information, this is the technology that's needed to compute it, and this is the data architecture that will structure and manage the relationships among all the various technologies.*

Missing from this process is an inquiry into the human require-ments: *How will this report be used? Who will have access to it?* Asking questions that might seem obvious can produce some surprising answers. For example, *How will people find this report? Is it clearly labeled?* After all, what good is a report if it's labeled with an obscure acronym that makes it almost impossible to locate? Posing ques-tions that range beyond the status quo can yield new benefits: *What other information might make this report more meaningful?* Responses to these questions can provide information that leads to innovation.

It's the job of the business requirements and the technical require-ments to tightly restrict what the software will do by narrowly defining transactions and the code that does the job—much of what is defined without ever being seen on a desktop screen. By its nature, this is a mechanical process that is insensitive to the limita-tions and the potential of variable, complex human beings. Unless the business and technical requirements are informed by human considerations, the finished product will roll off the assembly line, a piece of solid technology that fully complies with every business and technical requirement, before its fundamental deficiencies are discovered or its full potential can be explored. Only a broad investi-gation of requirements, one that anticipates the needs of the users, will give technologists the information they need to build a first-rate product.

AUTOMATING THE STATUS QUO

When we confine what we do to what we know, we minimize our oppor-tunities and replicate our experience—including our mistakes.

Whether a business specializes in pharmaceuticals or wealth management, its goals are simple: more, faster, better, and more profitable. Even in a peak year, it would be highly unusual to set a goal for the next fiscal year of achieving the same levels of productivity, sales, profits, and technical support. In each area, we want to see improvement.

Yet even though information technology is one of a company's biggest investments, much of what is spent on IT doesn't advance business goals. A vice president of Gartner, Inc. has estimated that "eight out of ten dollars that companies spend on IT is 'dead money'"—money that sustains the business and keeps the lights on but doesn't contribute to growth.

Speaking at the Gartner Symposium/ITxpo in Orlando, Florida, in October 2006, managing vice president Daryl Plummer said that IT investments allocated to changes that could transform the business are usually 20 percent or less, and he challenged business leaders and technologists to collaborate in an effort to double their investment in innovation.

Business leaders recognize that the key to innovation is new information, but when it comes to software they often fail to realize that even their best technical advisers may not be able to give them all the information they need to achieve the changes they want.

Many businesses run their operations with systems that have been built with multiple components acquired over a long period of time and haphazardly strung together piece by piece. When it's time to rebuild or replace the entire system, one approach is to make a record of every existing work process, inventory each function and feature of the legacy system, and create new technology to perform the same functions. But by relying exclusively upon the known, enormous opportunities are lost, including opportunities to create more efficient work processes and to present data more effectively.

Some developers of business-warehouse software would have you believe that if you can store all the data in one gigantic program, your business will be better; but a great deal of disappointment has been caused by confusing the retrieval of data with the delivery of information. Recently I was talking with the CEO of a company that produces software for the financial services industry, and he was telling me about his goals. His company's products are reliable and popular, but he was thinking about what the next level of performance might be: *Does the software present data in a form that is as clear as it could be? Are there new ways in which the data can be used?* And he wondered, *What would be the most efficient and cost-effective process to get the answers to those questions?*

Most of the software that does just so much (and no more) is the product of a development process that takes place within a closed circle of business and technology. This insular process produces software that can do nothing more than automate the status quo. Without the benefit of new information about existing work processes, people whose feet are firmly planted in the past and present are destined to produce an uninspired tool. Technically, software like this isn't dead, as Gartner has suggested—but regardless of how animated it may appear to be, it's not really alive. It haunts our desktops with the dead weight of the past, blocking our pathways to the future.

FROZEN IN THE ICU

In the autumn of 1999, an influential adviser to the federal government issued a somber report warning that "health care in the United States is not as safe as it should be—and can be" because of medical mistakes.

"To Err Is Human: Building a Safer Health System" was published by the Institute of Medicine, a nonprofit group that advises the government on health policy under a congressional charter granted to the National Academy of Sciences. The report cited estimates that at least 44,000 Americans, and perhaps as many as 98,000, die in U.S. hospitals each year because of medical errors that could have been prevented.

The study defined errors as "the failure of a planned action to be completed as intended or the use of a wrong plan to achieve an aim." One of the report's main findings was that most medical errors aren't caused by human carelessness. "More commonly," the report stated, "errors are caused by faulty systems, processes, and conditions that lead people to make mistakes or fail to prevent them." The report concluded that "mistakes can best be prevented by designing the health system at all levels to make it safer—to make it harder for people to do something wrong and easier for them to do it right."

In response, the Clinton administration created a task force, Congress held hearings, and public and private organizations initiated new research and development projects. The next year Congress appropriated $50 million to support efforts to reduce medical errors, and a coalition of corporations and nonprofits that provide health care benefits launched The Leapfrog Group, an organization dedicated to making "great leaps forward" in the quality of American health care.

As a first step to improve hospital safety, Leapfrog recommended that hospitals adopt computerized order entry systems for physicians' use in prescribing medications. The Institute of Medicine had found that "Medication errors now occur frequently in hospitals, yet many hospitals are not making use of known systems for improving safety, such as automated medication order entry systems." This emerging technology eliminates misinterpretation that can occur when physicians give verbal or written orders to nurses who must phone or fax them to other departments, and it also can alert physicians to common errors and dangerous drug interactions as they enter their orders. Leapfrog cited research showing that hospitals had been able to reduce serious errors in prescribing medication by more than 50 percent by using computerized physician order entry (CPOE).

Three years later, Children's Hospital of Pittsburgh (CHP) became one of the first pediatric hospitals in the country to install a computerized information management system for its physicians to use in virtually all inpatient care. One of the nation's top pediatric hospitals and one of the world's most active pediatric transplant centers, CHP has a staff that includes about 750 physicians who practice dozens of specialties.

The hospital's computerized order entry system, Children'sNet, was developed jointly by the hospital and a private company as part of a four-year, $10 million project to install a central electronic health record system. Children'sNet went live in October 2002, in an intensive six-day period in which physicians in nearly every department put aside their prescription pads and began ordering tests, medications, and treatments by using 1,300 computer terminals throughout the hospital. CHP praised the system as a giant leap forward.

"Even the most foolproof verbal and manual processes must compensate for human error. This system can only improve the safety and care for all of our patients," said Andrew Nowalk, M.D., Chief Medical Resident. "Children'sNet never forgets, misplaces, or tires, and it can 'be' everywhere at once." The *Pittsburgh Tribune-Review* hailed the system as "a prescription for accuracy."

Six months later, the hospital reported that prescription errors and transcription errors had plummeted. A later and more extensive study confirmed a significant decrease in medication mistakes, results that were consistent with findings by other hospitals that used similar systems.

But some physicians at CHP were seeing that new problems had arisen, and they wondered whether these problems might lead to unintended consequences. Yong Y. Han, M.D., a specialist in critical care, was frustrated and concerned about what was happening in the intensive care unit (ICU). In an article for *Pediatrics* co-authored with seven of his colleagues in 2005, Dr. Han described how the CPOE system had changed the chain of events as medical teams prepared for the arrival of seriously ill patients being transferred to the ICU from other hospitals:

Before implementation of CPOE, after radio contact with the transport team, the ICU fellow was allowed to order critical medications/drips, which then were prepared by the bedside ICU nurse in anticipation of patient arrival.... A full set of admission orders could be written and ready before patient arrival. After CPOE implementation, order entry was not allowed until after the patient had physically arrived... and been fully registered into the system, leading to potential delays in new therapies and diagnostic testing.

Not only were orders delayed, but the process of placing them also became much slower:

The physical process of entering stabilization orders often required an average of ten "clicks" on the computer mouse per order, which translated to ~1 to 2 minutes per single order as compared with a few seconds previously needed to place the same order by written form.

Most of the computer terminals were linked to the hospital's system via a wireless signal, and during peak periods the communications channel became clogged, creating even longer delays between each click of the mouse. Sometimes the computer screens froze.

Dr. Han observed that the new system also had changed the ways in which physicians and nurses interacted with patients:

Before CPOE implementation, physicians and nurses converged at the patient's bedside to stabilize the patient. After CPOE implementation, while one physician continued to direct medical management, a second physician was often needed solely to enter orders into the computer during the first fifteen minutes to one hour if a patient arrived in extremis.

Changes also were occurring in the way medicine was distributed. Once an order was placed,

bedside nurses were no longer allowed to grab critical medications from a satellite medication dispenser located in the ICU because as part of CPOE implementation, all medications... became centrally located within the pharmacy department. The priority to fill a medication order was assigned by the pharmacy department's algorithm. Furthermore, because pharmacy could not process medication orders until they had been activated, ICU nurses also spent significant amounts of time at a separate computer terminal and away from the bedside.

While pharmacists processed orders, other delays occurred. When doctors and nurses tried to view a patient record being used by one of the hospital's pharmacists, they were locked out and could not place new orders.

Dr. Han also was concerned that Children'sNet was reducing communication between doctors and nurses:

Before CPOE implementation, the physician expressed an intended order either through direct oral communication or by writing it at the patient's bedside (often reinforced with direct oral communication), with the latter giving the nurse a visual cue that a new order had been placed. The nurse had the opportunity to provide immediate feedback, which sometimes resulted in a necessary revision of that order. In addition, these face-to-face interactions often fostered discussions that were relevant to patient care and management.

After CPOE implementation, because order entry and activation occurred through a computer interface, often separated by several bed spaces or separate ICU pods, the opportunities for such face-to-face physician–nurse communication were diminished.

Despite the reduction in medication errors, Dr. Han and some of his colleagues began to question whether the ultimate outcome for patients was improving. They researched the records of 1,942 patients, including patients who had been admitted to the hospital during the 13 months just before implementation of the CPOE system and patients who had been admitted during the first five months afterward. What they found was disturbing.

In the months immediately following implementation of the CPOE system, the death rate had unexpectedly increased, rising from 2.8 percent (39 of 1,394 patients) in the 13 months before CPOE was implemented to 6.5 percent (36 of 548 patients) in the first five months after the system was implemented.

Dr. Han and his co-authors cautioned that no conclusions about cause and effect could be drawn from their study. Acknowledging that "it is difficult to assess the causality of increased mortality when a new intervention is given, especially when the intervention affects the administration of every drug given to every patient," they affirmed that "CPOE is an important medical information technology that holds great promise." But they warned that CPOE is a new technology, one that requires ongoing assessment of the ways in which patient care is affected by the "human-machine interface"— the highly sensitive point of contact between technology and the people it's meant to serve.

FIVE
THE RIGHT TEAM

It's easy to forget that our intimate daily interaction with computers is a relatively new relationship, but anyone who remembers the
1980s can recall the ways in which our workday world dramatically
changed.

By 1981, computer technology that had been developed to guide
military aircraft and submarines during World War II was being
routinely deployed for a myriad of commercial uses, and more than
a million computers of all sizes were in use in the United States.
As computers became more powerful, they also were becoming
smaller and more accessible, and workers whose experience with
computers had been limited to using a handheld calculator came
into their offices to discover a new machine the size of a TV sitting
on their desks. American companies were competing to build the
world's fastest supercomputers, and that year IBM also introduced

a personal computer that could be expanded to 256 kilobytes of memory. Business leaders and consumers alike were wondering how they could best make use of so much speed and power.

Each year, as businesses and consumers tried to keep up with the rapid developments in interactive media, fresh innovations followed. It was an exciting time. In 1985, when I was a freshman at Carnegie Mellon University (CMU), the more affluent students, myself not included, could be seen strolling across the quadrangle wearing headphones, listening to "Thriller" and "Born in the U.S.A." on their new $200 Sony Discman portable CD players. The year before, as the Los Angeles Raiders pounded the Washington Redskins at the Super Bowl in Tampa, Apple Computer had broadcast a futuristic commercial directed by Ridley Scott to introduce the Macintosh, the first successful mouse-driven computer with a graphical user interface. It seemed that almost anything might be possible.

Walkways and tradition join engineers with artists at CMU.

During my senior year at CMU I participated in an experimental project sponsored by the technology company NCR Corporation to design new uses for technology. The prototype that I designed—a touch-screen program to let prospective home buyers search listings of residential properties—gave me an entirely new outlook on what design could do, and I began to think about how my future career might relate to technology.

NCR's design project at CMU received some press, and when IBM came to campus to recruit, it seemed like the perfect opportunity. My interview went so well that at the end of the conversation, Tom Hardy, then one of IBM's design chiefs, asked, "What can we do to hire you?" I'd never traveled beyond the East Coast, so I said, "Well, I'd really like to work abroad." And he replied, "Is England far enough away?"

Obtaining a work visa in the United Kingdom was a challenge for a 21-year-old with no unique skills, so while I waited for my application to be approved I worked for a design firm in New York City. After eight months my papers came through, and one morning in the winter of 1990 I reported for work at IBM's Warwick Software Development Laboratory, a technology center located in a medieval town in the English countryside about 90 miles northwest of London. I was told that I was among the youngest recipients of a work visa in Britain, and I was the only designer working in the Warwick lab.

DESIGNING A NEW EXPERIENCE

The Warwick lab employed several hundred British computer scientists, many of whom were working on new applications for IBM's computer operating system, OS/2, which had been developed jointly by IBM and Microsoft two years earlier. Since then Microsoft had developed a competing system called Windows that was gaining popularity, and the Warwick lab was developing software for desktop computers that could be run by both Windows and OS/2. The lab also was working on another big project. IBM had developed a hugely successful decision-support business system called AS (Application System) that was running on mainframe computers at American Express and many other large companies, and the Warwick lab was adapting that software for desktop computers. The idea was to create charting and visual programming tools that nonspecialists could use to analyze data.

Proud history—
Warwick Castle,
like IBM's OS/2,
once dominated
the landscape.

I had almost no technology skills—beyond a working knowledge of Pascal that had been obligatory for every student at CMU, I couldn't write a line of code to save my life—so at first things didn't go well. I was asked to design icons. During my first few months at Warwick I must have created 300 icons for desktop toolbars: symbols for locating reports, editing reports, format-ting reports, saving reports, and printing reports. It became clear that unless I found a way to make myself more valuable, I'd be designing icons until I was blue in the face, and I'd never have any meaningful impact on the way the software actually performed. But I had two lucky breaks.

By sheer chance, I'd landed in a lab run by a visionary: Tony Temple was a systems engineer who had led the development of AS before becoming director of the lab, and later he became vice president of IBM's global Ease of Use program and an IBM Fellow. Tony under-stood that if software tools were to reach a broader market, they needed to be easy to use—in fact, they needed to be beautiful and desirable. To make that happen, Tony was energetically promoting this philosophy throughout IBM, trying to influence every depart-ment in the United States and the United Kingdom, and he used my design expertise as just one of the tools in his big bag of tricks. He would be in the States working on a new project, and then he would come back to Warwick and say, "Harold, here's what they're trying to do, but I don't think this is the right way to do it. Give me some ideas." Together we'd brainstorm and sift through the possibilities.

At the same time I realized that I had two powerful allies among my colleagues. The lab had two human factors analysts who were responsible for testing the usability of IBM's new software, and their PhDs in psychology gave them considerable clout among the engineers and programmers. These two researchers were respon-sible for predicting how well the software we were building would perform in the hands of its users, and I found that the three of us liked to ask the same questions:

Who will be using this software? How much experience do they have in using similar technology? What will they need to learn? Will they under-stand the instructions and error messages? When they make a mistake, what will they need to do to correct it? Which tasks will they be perform-ing most often? How long does it take them to complete these tasks? How will they use the data they obtain? Will they want to circulate that information to others? How can this software help them do their jobs more effectively?

The two psychologists with whom I worked at IBM's Warwick lab had the academic training and the scientific tools to conduct the design research that would answer these questions. Through trial runs and video monitoring they tested, measured, and analyzed the performance of users on every task, on every screen, pinpointing the places where people made mistakes and identifying communications gaps and blind alleys that were sabotaging the brilliant technology. Through observation, interviews, and questionnaires, they were able to evaluate how well the quality of the user experience matched the technical quality of the product.

Once the human factors analysts had identified problem areas, they might make recommendations for changes, but they were not designers. Sometimes it was the job of this designer to propose solutions that could be executed by the programmers, but I was only one person, so other times usability problems were simply pointed out to the programmers and they were left to fix these issues to the best of their abilities—the same abilities that had brought them to this point. If a solution was impossible within time limitations, training would have to do for the time being, and we would schedule a fix for a subsequent release.

The human factors analysts and I covered as many bases as we could, and soon we began to work as a unit. Our greatest challenge was our position in the development cycle—at the end. Once code is developed, change is always difficult and expensive. As a designer, I kept thinking that our moment of influence within the software development process was like that of an architect who hasn't been allowed to visit a construction site until a building has been completed and everything but the wallpaper, carpets, and furniture has been installed. At the Warwick lab, there was no end to the issues that our professional eyes could see at a glance, but unfortunately there was little that could be done to remedy them other than changes to surfaces. It became obvious that our value would be realized if our work began earlier in the development process, with cognitive and behavioral scientists providing insightful recommendations to software developers and a designer rapidly sketching innovative alternatives to how a software application could appear and behave on-screen.

THE SCIENCE OF COMMON SENSE

Technology is worthless unless it empowers the people who use it, so it makes sense to balance the needs of business, technology, and people. But because these needs usually conflict, the software development process often becomes a battle for control between business and technology.

Without the presence of designers and other professionals who have the expertise—and the responsibility—to think objectively and creatively about how to mediate those conflicts, either business or technology will win by forcing through a lopsided resolution. When there's just one winner, everyone loses, but a process that seeks equilibrium among the needs of business, technology, and human beings can deliver a solution that yields substantial business benefits.

The first step is to ask what the business software needs to do.

Most executives, if asked to list the software tools they need to run their operations more effectively, could describe exactly what they want. In fact, every business leader who participates in the process of acquiring business software has experience in defining and specifying those requirements. So why is it that even businesses with extensive financial and technical resources have so much trouble getting the quality of software they need? The most common complaint I hear from executives goes something like this: "We asked our people to tell us what they wanted, and we built a system that does everything they said they needed, and now no one seems to like it. We've trained everyone on the system, and they're still not using it. We can't figure out what's causing the problem."

Usually, these systems do 80 percent of what people expect, but they don't do it in the *way* that people expect. Almost always, what's missing is sensitivity to the user interface, the point at which people touch the thing—consideration of whether the language displayed on the screen uses words and names that people recognize and whether information is organized in a way that is clear and predictable.

Since my time at Warwick, I've learned that when designers and scientists who specialize in human factors participate in a project from the start, they can listen to the stated needs of a business or user community, observe work processes and see how tasks are performed, and form an accurate picture of what is genuinely needed. Compared with the typical survey of end users and an inventory of things a business *wants* from a new tool, the understanding of people and organizations that human factors experts can contribute represents a dramatically improved definition of what's required of a computer system—and what's *needed* by its human users.

More recently, business analysts have come to serve as intermediaries between the workers in an organization and the technologists who are ready to deliver the software application. These individuals may have a more objective view of the business and its needs, but like the business professionals and executives before them, they lack the training to understand the human component of the software's definition and to specify requirements that skillfully balance business processes and methods with a realistic assessment of human abilities and performance. Business analysts possess a clear understanding of the business, but their knowledge is incomplete.

Designers and psychologists may seem like unlikely candidates to involve in the definition of a business system. But these professionals possess skills and techniques to provide commonsense insights that would otherwise go undetected, insights that fill a tremendous gap in the knowledge that drives most software development. Traditionally, deep knowledge of business process has been the framework upon which detailed descriptions of business systems are created and from which software code is written. But when we focus on business process alone, we ignore the humans who are responsible for connecting this computing technology to the work of the business. This scenario fails to address an entire stratum of requirements, needs defined by the community of human beings who perform all the routine tasks of business as well as the communities of individuals who are our customers.

A TENDENCY TO CRASH

One day in 1945, on an island in the Pacific more than four thousand miles west of Honolulu, a young U.S. Army Air Forces pilot watched as an American transport plane approached for a landing.

The plane was a C-46 Commando, one of the primary cargo and troop-carrier aircraft of World War II. Its nickname was "the whale," and it was big enough and strong enough to carry five tons of cargo, including Jeeps and light planes. Lieutenant Stanley N. Roscoe saw the plane touch down smoothly on the coral runway—but then it "appeared to settle under the surface like a submarine starting to submerge," as he later wrote. Roscoe saw sparks, and then an explosion. Suddenly he realized what had happened: After touchdown, the copilot had pulled up the wheels instead of raising the flaps.

Roscoe had no way of knowing that the catastrophe he had just witnessed wasn't unusual. But as he later learned, it was part of a pattern.

More than a year earlier, military commanders had noticed that the term *pilot error* was appearing in accident reports for certain aircraft. As Lieutenant Roscoe later recalled in an article describing the events, military leaders had asked an American psychologist, Lieutenant Alphonse Chapanis, to figure out why pilots and copilots of P-47, B-17, and B-25 bombers were making the mistake of retracting the wheels instead of raising the flaps after landing. When Lieutenant Chapanis examined the cockpits of these planes, he saw that the wheels and the flaps were controlled by adjacent levers or toggle switches that looked identical. He also discovered that the corresponding controls on another plane, the C-47, looked different and were separated from one another—and that the pilots of those aircraft were not confusing the two.

Chapanis realized that many so-called pilot errors were errors in design. As a temporary solution, a small wheel was attached to the end of the wheel control on many of these aircraft and a wedge-shaped attachment was added to the flap control. After the war, these shape-coded controls were standardized for aircraft around the world.

During World War II the term *engineering psychology* hadn't yet been coined, but psychologists and engineers collaborated to invent the science as they scrambled to correct problems on newly designed aircraft that been rushed through production with little testing. In the years immediately after the war, through support by the U.S. Department of Defense, the study of human behavior in the operation of systems began to flourish at military labs and at universities throughout the country, generating a new surge of research. Much of this research was carried out by psychologists whose interest in systems design had been influenced by their military experience. Alphonse Chapanis joined the psychology department at Johns Hopkins University and produced an influential book that became the first textbook on engineering psychology. Stanley Roscoe became the first student at a fledgling program in aviation psychology at the University of Illinois, and his research on the relationship between instrument design and pilot performance led to many innovations in aviation training and navigation technology.

As the military's new approach to systems design spread to the private sector, other industries began to look more closely at the compatibility of their machines with their human operators, and a specialty began to emerge. In 1957 a group of 90 psychologists, physiologists, engineers, and other professionals in southern California banded together to form the Human Factors Society of America to promote the study of how humans interact with technology. By the 1980s, human factors analysts were working with business and government to help develop transportation systems, medical equipment, communications networks, public safety systems, new models of automobiles and other consumer products, and software for the emerging industry of information technology.

Wheels up—
This C-46 had
a rough landing.

DESIGNERS AND THE ART OF INTERPRETATION

For most of us who grew up in the United States, our formal education in art, and perhaps therefore our understanding of it, ends somewhere around fourth grade. This may account for the common misunderstanding of what design is.

In my 20 years of experience in the design field, I have observed that when people say, "That's a really cool design," they probably mean that they like the *look* of an object—its curves, its color, its texture, or another stylistic characteristic. Conversely, I seldom hear people say, "That's a really cool design" when they swiftly update their daily calendars and personal contacts, move smoothly through a self-service checkout line at a hardware superstore, or successfully navigate the subway of a foreign city. Too often, our understanding of design is limited to its physical form and doesn't extend to the quality of our experience with that form.

At first glance, Target's distinctive prescription bottle, with its irregular, flattened shape and bold red color, so different from the decades-old tradition of amber cylinders, may look like nothing more than a company's effort to differentiate itself from its competitors, and indeed Target has done well representing its brand with quirky images and a strict use of the color red. However, it is the experience we have with this form and this color that demonstrates the real impact of design. What the designer has presented is a container that serves the same old function, to house pills. But unlike previous forms of prescription bottles, it also provides a flat surface upon which labels and instructions can more easily be read, reducing the risk that important messages will be overlooked or misunderstood. The color and shape of this object displayed on a shelf might draw the admiring comment, "Cool design!"—but those who take it home and use it will enjoy all the practical advantages of a product that truly embodies good design.

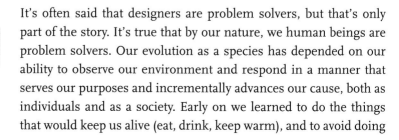

Better data display: A label on a cylinder can be hard to read, but Target's design minimizes risk.

It's often said that designers are problem solvers, but that's only part of the story. It's true that by our nature, we human beings are problem solvers. Our evolution as a species has depended on our ability to observe our environment and respond in a manner that serves our purposes and incrementally advances our cause, both as individuals and as a society. Early on we learned to do the things that would keep us alive (eat, drink, keep warm), and to avoid doing

things that might hurt us (avoid certain poisonous plants and ber-
ries, steer clear of that lion). Over time our goals advanced beyond
simply staying alive to an interest in doing things that make us feel
good, finding ways to decrease our labor, and working to control
our environment. Our problem-solving abilities have enabled us to
craft tools both simple and complex that allow us to till the earth,
build lighted cities, and traverse the planet within hours.

When we think of design as problem solving, it's easy to assume
that in some way all of us are designers. This is like concluding that
because our instinct for self-preservation leads us to routinely act
on the knowledge that medical research brings us—we take vita-
mins to boost our immune systems, try to avoid certain germs not
visible to the human eye, and eat nutritious foods—in some way
we're all physicians. But just being able to take care of our basic
physiological needs doesn't make us physicians, and even though
we each possess a certain natural level of problem-solving ability,
we're not all designers.

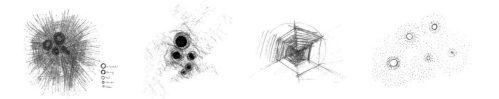

My education taught me that design is process. It's a way of
seeing, thinking, and acting that allows for the creation of the
most appropriate forms to provide a human audience with the
best possible experiences. Design is not an outcome; it's a means
to a successful outcome. Designers are professionals who specialize in solving problems by creating new objects, by improving
old objects, or by making old objects disappear. They're trained
to use their hands to connect an idea hovering in their brains,
or a concept shared by a team of brains, with a sheet of paper
laid out before them in a way that transcends the materials and
the process of making marks. Designers allow us to understand
a vision of a new object or a new system and to participate in its
refinement and its realization.

Thinking it through—
Before a line of code
is written, in seconds
a designer's sketches
can show how groups of
data and features might
be organized in several
locations within a
software application, and
how users could navigate
within them.

Show me a well-trained designer and I will show you an exceptional listener, an attentive observer, an explorer, a risk taker, and a highly capable communicator. Architects, industrial designers, graphic designers, and interface designers all share a commitment to a centuries-old process of design, a rigorous process of discovery, understanding, consensus building, and production.

LOOKING AT A PROJECT FROM EVERY ANGLE

These days, designs for sports stadiums, automobiles, and most other consumer products are executed with the help of computer-assisted design (CAD) software that can rotate a drawing 360 degrees, create 3-D views, and slice each view into an infinite number of cross sections to preview the final form. Designers who came of age before the invention of these electronic tools used pencil and paper to perform the same tests.

When I was a sophomore at Carnegie Mellon, CMU's Steve Stadelmeier asked my sophomore design studio to imagine a 3-D shape. He then asked us to draw it dozens of times rotated in space. Then he asked us to visualize three copies of the same shape intersecting one another and to draw this complex situation dozens of times from as many different vantage points. Finally, we were asked to build cardboard models of the intersecting forms we had just drawn.

The ability to imagine the invisible, to visualize its final form from every angle, and to clearly portray that form to an audience is one of the unique skills that a designer brings to any problem-solving exercise.

A designer's first job is to understand what needs to be designed and for whom. This isn't a passive step of taking an order from a client; it's a process of gathering essential information to challenge and verify the client's assumptions, with the goal of discovering what factors haven't been considered as project parameters.

To fill the gaps in the definition of the project, a designer gathers information from multiple sources so that the starting point is the most accurate and complete definition of the challenge. These data inputs may include a designer's direct observations of some of the people who will be using the product as well as the environment in

Imagining the possibilities—These sketches show how three simple
3-D shapes might be arranged in relation to one another. Designers use
a similar process to test alternative ideas when they create prototypes
for data-visualization tools.

which the proposed device will be used, together with the research of psychologists, anthropologists, and technologists—all in an effort to understand the limitations and the possibilities of the project's context and to prove the accuracy of the project's definition. This period is comparable to an attorney's pretrial discovery process, in which a deep and broad exploration of information defines the framework for strategies that will unfold during trial. The attorney doesn't just take the client's word. Nor does an attorney assume that any one expert or witness owns the truth.

In software development, the very definition of what needs to be coded by programmers is typically flawed, because this definition is the result of surveys and polling conducted under the assumption that target audiences can accurately and effectively articulate their needs. They cannot. Most people can only describe what they want, based on their understanding of their own histories and their current situations. Delivering on stated wants will miss delivering on most of their needs, and almost always will stifle opportunities for innovation. Equally inaccurate is the assumption that individuals deeply knowledgeable of their particular field are qualified to design tools for it.

If you had asked my grandfather what kind of car he wanted when he was ready to replace his Model T, he might have asked for a car with a better set of tools, but what he really needed was a car that wouldn't require him to keep a set of tools handy to make routine adjustments. Poll a sampling of today's drivers about what they want in their next car, and you're likely to hear everything from reasonable requests for better mileage to absurd desires for triple the power and double the speed. Deliver on all these lists of wants, and lives will be lost. This is essentially how businesses specify software requirements all the time—by listing superficially desirable features and functions without challenging the genesis of these requirements or even their value before handing them to systems developers to build.

Translating an accurate definition of need into a physical form is an intricate step in the design of any product. Designers are uniquely qualified to do this because they can quickly and effectively produce drawings, models, and prototypes to describe physical forms that will meet the defined requirements for a proposed system. These visual tools provide early, affordable opportunities to see and experience what could be. Most importantly, they allow any number of individuals the opportunity to contribute valuable information that can influence and refine the design.

Exploration and discovery—an accurate statement of need to drive a project, the definition and refinement of a physical form through iteration of collaboration and adjustment, and the delivery of a proven specification to produce the object—this is the process of design, the sequence of steps and the communication model of which the designer is the trained steward. The most beautiful and the most useful physical forms created by human hands, from our skyscrapers and cathedrals to our wristwatches and mobile phones, have come about through this design process. Designers allow us to clearly understand a problem, efficiently explore the possibilities, and map a path to the realization of that vision.

INFORM → DISCOVER → SKETCHING → REFINEMENT → SPECIFICATION → PRODUCTION → EVALUATION

In the design process, the definition of a problem is followed by iterations of sketching and refinement to validate the concept and achieve consensus.

THE OTHER CUSTOMERS

For two years during the late 1990s I had the pleasure of working on the development of new information technology for health care, and during my time with this project I learned something interesting about how manufacturers of large software systems choose to involve their customers in the strategic evolution of their products.

At that time I was designing the user interface for one of the earliest applications to store patient records using a graphical user interface, and I was lucky enough to be invited to work with a team of former McDonnell Douglas software developers who had joined First Data Corporation's Health Systems Group in Charlotte, North Carolina. The folks from McDonnell Douglas were talented and highly experienced, and it was exhilarating to think what new tools we might be able to create.

Because of the highly specialized nature of the system to be built, the organization was aware of the importance of guidance from professionals in the health care field. But this input came not from potential users of the system but from a few former health care professionals who were members of the development team and from buyers and potential buyers channeled to us by the sales team. These proxies for potential users who could contribute genuine understanding and insight presented an ongoing challenge to an already complex development process. The quality of their input was continually challenged by the technologists who held the reins of the project and who often considered any other viewpoint as just another opinion.

Over the years the software industry has made efforts to involve all its customers—buyers as well as the end users of its products—in the design and development of systems. Unfortunately, customers can be demanding, unpredictable, and contradictory, which makes them highly problematic sources of guidance for system design. Software developers have wisely understood that such involvement can lead to tremendous confusion and lack of focus, so a technique called the user group was created in an attempt to manage input from this potentially uncontrollable mob. Essentially, this technique is designed to retard input, to demonstrate what the system manufacturer has already committed to build, and to seek high-level confirmation that the developers are on the right track.

The tradition of the user group persists, and I remain fascinated by its resilience within the industry despite its profound ineffectiveness. User group sessions are fun, for sure—sometimes hosted by a software manufacturer in an exotic locale with lots of entertainment, food, and booze, with a few hours of presentation in a room lined with chairs where presenters talk about what's coming next for the product, lead a walk-through of the product's new features, and take an obligatory survey of the audience to gather input and approval. Those who represent the software company at these meetings are mostly salespeople, and what they bring back to the company from these events is erroneously seen as valuable customer input for the future of the product.

Members of the audience at a user group session are customers, but they're typically not the people who will use the system. Of course, they represent the users—they will be making the purchasing decision for their organizations—but even when the buyers of a large clinical enterprise system are doctors, they usually are not the doctors or the nurses who will be using the system. And what is presented to this audience may not be an opportunity to *use* the system, but rather an opportunity to see it demonstrated by an expert. The experience is comparable to watching Martha Stewart prepare a 25-pound turkey in puff pastry in a carefully orchestrated process, making it seem so easy that anyone could do it.

Just as members of a user group usually aren't the most qualified judges of a system, the collection of professionals who *run* these meetings aren't well suited to the task of impartially gathering and analyzing responses from their audiences. Typically, the presenters are product managers seeking direction for the evolution of their applications and confirmation that the latest development is a good one, and sales representatives who are doing what they need to do—move product. Not one of these folks is well suited to elicit a genuine definition of user needs or to translate these descriptions into product designs. But when designers and psychologists manage input from appropriate audiences, it's unlikely that the effort will be sidetracked by impractical wish lists or inappropriate goals thrust forward by a demanding audience.

Not long ago I spoke with the CIO of a large health care network who was about to purchase an enterprise system to compile and store medical records that would be used by hundreds of physicians—radiologists, internists, pediatricians, neurologists, hematologists, cardiologists, and all the other specialists within the network—as well as every member of their support staffs. The CIO and his team had nearly completed their evaluation of competing systems, and the network's CEO had asked my company to consult with him on the purchasing decision. The projected cost of this system was $185 million.

My first question to the CIO was whether he could add to the list of criteria the quality of usability, and he replied, "We've done that. The companies are giving demos of their products for groups of doctors, nurses, and users from admissions, pharmacy, and every other department, and these representative users are going to watch the demos to see how the workflows will be structured to see if they have any issues with them."

"That's great," I said, "but won't it be better if an expert could look at each of these systems individually to see how intuitive it is, whether it follows a logical sequence, and how clearly its user interface is designed, independent of the workflows?"

And he said, "That's not necessary—we're expert enough."

"With all due respect," I said, "You're the CIO. You know technology, and I'm sure you know a lot about this business, but I don't think we could say that you're representative of these users."

"You'd be surprised," he said. "For instance, let's talk about radiology."

Thinking that the CIO might be uniquely qualified, I asked, "Excuse me, are you a radiologist?"

"No," he responded, "but I've been around hospitals and hospital systems for 20 years, and I know what they need. I've purchased and implemented several radiology systems during my career, and I know more about those systems and what they can do than the radiologists."

I said, "But you're looking for a tool that will fit well into their hands, and frankly, your hands aren't their hands. You need an independent voice to translate the actions and goals of these specialists into the system's features and design characteristics."

The CIO was unmoved. "I will give them the system they need," he insisted.

"Based on your knowledge of other systems?" I asked. He said, "Yes."

If system design is based on assumptions, where does innovation come from? If your knowledge is limited to what you have experienced and what you have directly observed, your imagination will be reined in. Even your own observations may have marginal value unless you've been trained to observe, record, and analyze human behavior. For example, do your observations lead you to find out: *Exactly how do these people perform their work?* Do they lead you to discover: *Why do they work the way they do?*

Gathering information from users as well as buyers needn't be complex or problematic, and it doesn't have to be expensive. There's no need to fly to Las Vegas or Miami to assemble in a hotel conference room. Design researchers can meet customers where they are, and in fact they prefer to work this way. In the field they can watch, listen, and document what is described to them, and they also can record a genuine understanding of what will be needed from a system by individuals who perform specific tasks, in certain places, in order to help them meet and exceed business goals.

Too often, software developers have failed to distinguish between the customers who write the checks and the customers who ultimately will be served by the system. Without satisfying the buyers, money doesn't move and the system never gets off the shelf. For this reason, most business technology caters to just one group of customers, resulting in well-intentioned software development processes that reflect little appreciation for the differences between the needs of its two very different constituencies.

ANALYZING THE WORKFLOW

To show how a medical team at a hospital responds when a patient experiences a crisis, a standard workflow diagram might be a series of boxes and arrows representing the actions and decision points of the business process. In contrast, the diagram below, made by a design researcher and an anthropologist, records the sequence of human actions and interactions as well as their timing and locations.

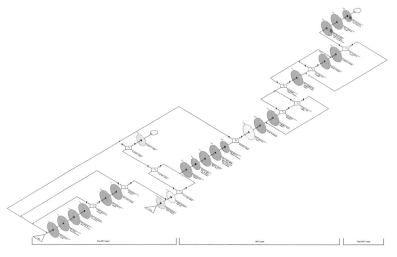

Below, human-centered workflow diagrams record the actions of a Nursing Care Coordinator (NCC) one afternoon from 12:30 to 2 p.m. to show how she interacts with a dozen other professionals.

At right, a close-up of the middle diagram shows how the NCC is observed assisting the patient and preparing paperwork while interacting with other members of the team, who are shown in arcs radiating to the left.

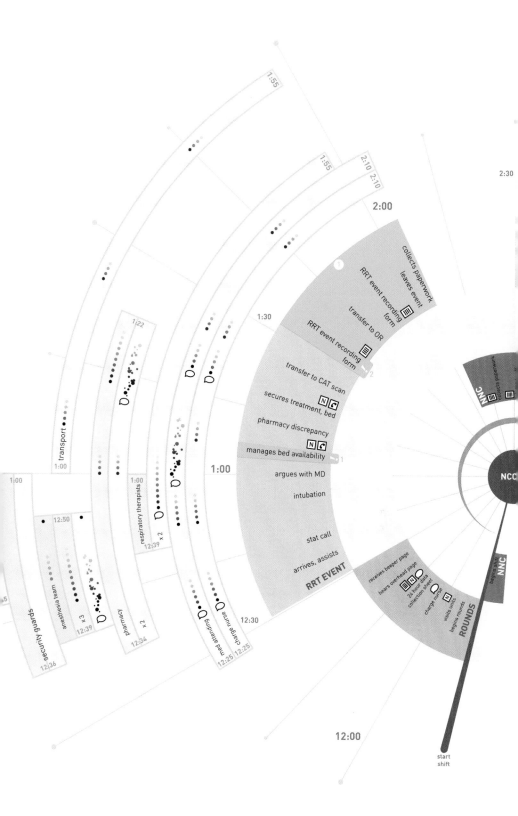

2:30

1:55

2:10 2:10

2:00

collects paperwork
leaves event
RRT event recording form
transfer to OR
1:30
RRT event recording form
transfer to CAT scan
secures treatment, bed
pharmacy discrepancy
manages bed availability
argues with MD
intubation
stat call
arrives, assists
RRT EVENT

1:55

1:22

transport
1:00

1:00
respiratory therapists
x 2
12:39

1:00

12:50

anesthesia team
x 3
12:39

security guards
12:36

pharmacy
x 2
12:34

12:25 12:25

med attending nurse
charge nurse

12:30

receives beeper page
hears overhead page
24 hour data collection sheet
charge nurse
visits units
begins rounds
ROUNDS

NNC

NCC

NCC
begins shift

NNC

collects paperwork

1:00

12:00

start
shift

Asking a group of people to sit in a conference room and describe how they work while a facilitator draws flowcharts on a whiteboard will inevitably produce a series of intricate corporate fairy tales.

If you were to ask your sales reps to describe how they prepare their expense reports, they might tell you that they use certain programs to submit them electronically on the first of the month, but they may have become so accustomed to working their way through a cumbersome process that they don't think to mention that every month it takes them 45 minutes because the system requires them to toggle back and forth between two programs. If you were to ask them how the process could be improved, they probably would tell you that it needs to be faster— but if you convey that requirement to IT, your CIO might tell you that the system already is operating at maximum speed and that your sales reps just need a little more training in using the programs.

One of the most valuable contributions that designers and psychologists can make to a business system is to effectively involve buyers and users in the design and development process. Through direct observation and the use of scientific data-gathering techniques, designers and psychologists can study and measure the behavior of representative men and women in the context of the system's eventual deployment. Observation shows us what is happening, and allows us to understand how things are actually working (or not working).

Early in my career I was asked to lead the design of a new user interface for a call-center application that was being used by telephone operators in a credit card company. I joined this project at a point when system requirements were being gathered from business stakeholders and end users. According to so-called best practice, the phone operators and their bosses had been assembled in a room lined with whiteboards, and a facilitator was engaged to lead the room of people through several hours of questioning about their jobs and the system that supported them.

Among the requirements for the new system that had already been documented was the number of open data fields that the new system would need to display on the screen to record the telephone numbers of every credit card holder: eight! *Wow,* I thought, *I must lead a very plain existence.* Was it possible that most of their customers had eight phone numbers? It just didn't make sense, so I arranged to visit the call center to watch and listen. As I looked over the shoulder of one operator, I saw that in fact the screen before us displayed eight open spaces labeled "telephone number."

When I asked why so many phone numbers would be stored for each customer, the operator explained that two or three numbers were all that were needed, and that the other data fields were used to store the customer's account password, mother's maiden name, and various other names and numbers. All these data fields were labeled "telephone number," and the operators patiently filled in the rest of the information wherever they could. What the operators wanted, and what they asked for, was enough space to record every bit of information they were responsible for gathering—but what they needed was a better system.

Seeing these individuals in the context of their work revealed an unstated need, but it also revealed that the business had changed since that last system's deployment, and this jerry-rigging of the displays was a manifestation of the change. More questions could now be asked and more accuracy could be gained: *What is the additional information that is keyed into all these fields? When is it gathered from the customer? Why? How is it used?*

```
------------------ACCOUNT SETUP------------(v.2)-
                Enter Card Holder Information
--------------------------------------------------------
  COMMAND INPUT ===> _                      page Up/Down
--------------------------------------------------------

  Telephone Number 1:          Telephone Number 5:

  (555)-555-5555               picnic

  Telephone Number 2:          Telephone Number 6:

  Robert                       0561654654489

  Telephone Number 3:          Telephone Number 7:

  Smith                        California

  Telephone Number 4:          Telephone Number 8:

  Williams                     90071█
--------------------------------------------------------

  F1=Help   F3=Exit   F10=Actions   F12=Cancel
```

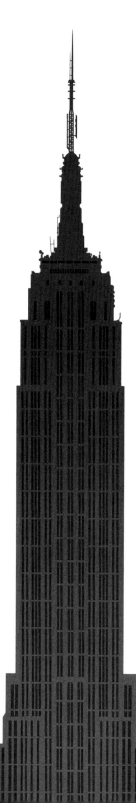

By consensus, a singular vision—
the Empire
State Building

A POWERFUL PARTNERSHIP

Proposing that business executives collaborate with psychologists, anthropologists, designers, programmers, and end users may sound like a dangerous way to design and build anything, especially a complex business tool. But the sorry state of most business systems tells us precisely how much we have yet to learn from the way in which we have successfully engaged in the design and construction of other complex systems.

If an architect were unable to lead the delivery of a skyscraper, imagine the lack of vision, understanding, and knowledge that would plague the construction process. Blueprints—the most meaningful expression of an architect's vision, and ultimately the rule book for construction—would not exist. Instead, the builder would be forced to work from the next best means of communication: written and verbal descriptions of what the welders, glazers, electricians, plumbers, and a host of other craftspeople should deliver in the final product. Ridiculous? Impossible? Absolutely.

A blueprint is the instruction manual for the creation of every square inch of a building. But it isn't the blueprint itself that is valuable. It's what the blueprint enables—a singular, common vision that is endorsed and proven by a variety of expert voices, each focused on a different facet of the system. Each facet must be sound in itself, but it also must be compatible with the configuration and the needs of every other system, and together they must work in unison to comprise the overall integrity of the building.

SIX

FIND OUT WHAT YOU REALLY NEED

Early in my career I had the good fortune to work side by side with a remarkable man who had a very clear view of what computers can and can't do.

My colleague, Ming Zhang, was a brilliant computer scientist who had been working in China when Communist Party leader Chairman Mao announced the start of the Cultural Revolution in 1966. In an effort to create a new society in which peasants and intellectuals would be equals, Chairman Mao closed the schools and ordered millions of young people into the countryside to do manual labor. Many professionals were arrested, and Dr. Zhang was imprisoned in a salt mine. Years later, when the Cultural Revolution collapsed, he was released, and he immigrated to the United States.

I met Dr. Zhang in 1993, when we both were working for First Data Corporation in Charlotte, North Carolina. We were developing a new computerized medical record system for hospitals, the first system to offer a graphical user interface in which doctors and nurses could record and view their notes. Dr. Zhang was writing the code, and I was designing the interface that would be the point of contact for people who used the system. To find out how the display could best support tasks such as recording the administration of medication, noting vital signs, and adding doctors' notes, I would meet regularly with a nursing professional, and once this nurse and I felt that we were on the right track, I would meet with Ming to assess the technical feasibility of the designs we had created.

My desk happened to be near his, and several times each day we'd review proposed designs to display the clinical data. His mantra rings in my head to this day: "Harold, we can make computers do anything—all things are possible with code. But we need to make them do the right thing. It's just a matter of where you want to spend your dime."

Nowhere is this more evident than in the world of business systems. It really does seem possible that whatever one can imagine a business needing from a system, developers and engineers are quite capable of delivering. It's a question of where you want to spend your dime (or many millions of dimes). The challenge is no longer a question of whether we can make a computer perform a certain function or store a specific array of data. The question now is figuring out what we really need all of this computing technology to do for us in order for our organizations to achieve their goals. Presently we're buying so-called solutions—enterprise resource planning, dashboards, customer-relationship management, data warehouses, and portals, all impressive technological feats. But are these really solutions? Not unless they genuinely satisfy a need and deliver results to the bottom line. All too often, we're buying what's available, not what's needed.

When we build bespoke systems within an organization, the way in which we define system requirements must extend beyond an inventory of functions and data. A set of requirements must not simply reflect an understanding of what the business does; it also must clearly reflect an understanding how the organization must perform and how the system requirements will meet the needs of the business and its human constituents.

THE CORRECT DEFINITION

Understanding what system you need to build or buy is typically based on a definition of business processes. These processes are usually defined as the optimal sequence of decisions and actions to support efficiency and to benefit the bottom line. However, this is an incomplete picture.

The communities of human beings who will execute these business processes have their own set of information to contribute to the project definition. The effectiveness of a business system is directly tied to whether its human workforce can effectively engage in its execution, and the best-laid plans for system efficiency can run terribly awry unless we understand the potential, the abilities, the experiences, and the goals of the people responsible for delivering on these plans. Every business needs a system that will help its human workforce to efficiently and effectively perform. Instead, most of the time what we have is technology that managers wrongly believe they can use to *make* that workforce deliver efficiency.

Underlying the business process and technical plans are human processes— workers whose individual jobs will have needs not identified in the business requirements.

To define what's needed from a system, it's important to look at what you have. Existing processes, systems—and people—can reveal a great deal about what is good, and not so good, in the current landscape. Unfortunately, too many businesses fail to examine the effectiveness of their current systems.

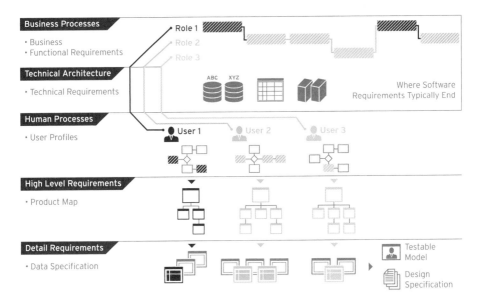

Although the financial services industry and some other sectors of the business community have been receptive to new ways in which technology makes it possible to gain actionable insights from data's transformation to information, other members of the business community remain fixated on traditional ways of displaying data, especially within the health care industry. For example, for decades every patient occupying a hospital bed had an associated patient record, a pen-and-pencil, paper-based record that tracked the patient's treatment and served as the main conduit of communication among a team of caregivers during the patient's hospital stay. The patient record has a standardized format to organize and record information, and in it is a sheet of heavy paper that usually unfolds to extend beyond the 8.5×11–inch page dimension of the basic document. This is the nursing flow sheet, where nurses note their observations and measurements of the patient's condition and record interventions and assessments, organized according to time and date. Within the patient record this is the nurses' turf. No one else providing care to the patient writes on this page, and doctors will write their notes elsewhere.

I've participated in several computerizations of the nursing flow sheet, and in these projects a nurse usually leads the product design process by translating the paper-based record to on-screen requirements for data display and system functionality—a computerization of the current method. Whenever a question arises as to the correctness of modeling the new world according to such a strict translation of the old, nerves become raw and concerns of user adoption and acceptance drown out any challenges to this approach: "Nurses understand the flow sheet, so that's what we need to deliver."

In Philadelphia, where my company is headquartered, there's no shortage of hospitals, and recently I talked about medical records with an expert on the subject. F. Philip Robin is a practicing lawyer who also is a physician, and he has a long and successful record of winning medical malpractice suits. My company had just begun a project to design yet another nursing flow sheet application, and I thought that it would be worthwhile to ask him about the logic and wisdom of recording data in this fashion, with doctors and nurses quite literally on separate pages. He smiled and said that in fact, the very design of the patient chart—the way in which data is recorded and assessed by caregivers—is at the root of his successful record of litigation. He told me that he could examine almost any patient chart and identify a point where communication between caregivers broke down, and he pointed to the nursing flow sheet as a primary culprit.

Dr. Robin describes the structure of the patient chart as a collection of separate and distinct narratives. If we consider the patient chart as a developing story of a patient's care, its structure dictates that multiple parallel stories evolve over time. What we understand about the patient's care will depend on what narrative we choose to follow and when. Physicians create and monitor a narrative that is separate from those of the nurses, the radiologists, and the laboratory technicians. Over lunch recently a hospital administrator who is also a physician responded to this story by explaining that in his facility, one of his concerns with a new electronic medical record that does a fine job of capturing and storing nursing notes is that the notes are never actually being read by others during the patient's treatment.

And here we were, designing another flow sheet—one projected onto a computer screen with better organization and more clearly presented data, but a flow sheet nonetheless. Under these circumstances, the correct requirements for a new system that correlates all data and alerts caregivers to any conflict, discrepancies, or errors will never be articulated. And unfortunately, that unified patient-care narrative is quite often only fully understood much later, when it's too late.

Meeting the challenge of delivering a computerized nursing flow sheet is no project definition at all. It's simply an exercise in delivering technological capability. Of course we can make a computer replicate a flow sheet—after all, "all things are possible with code"—but should we? When it comes to defining what we really need from a business system, the answer lies beyond an inventory of functions and data. The answer lies within a complete understanding of the business—the processes, the information, and the people.

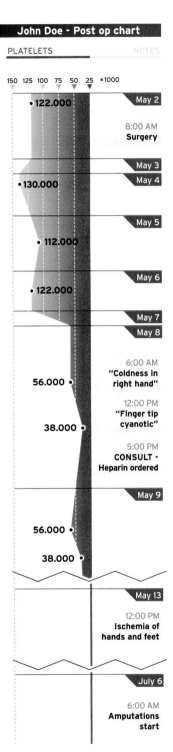

John Doe - Post op chart

PLATELETS   NOTES

150 125 100 75 50 25 ×1000

• **122.000**   May 2

                       8:00 AM
                       Surgery

                       May 3
• **130.000**   May 4

                       May 5
• **112.000**

                       May 6
• **122.000**

                       May 7
                       May 8

                       6:00 AM
                       "Coldness in
 56.000 •   **right hand"**

                       12:00 PM
                       "Finger tip
 38.000 •   **cyanotic"**

                       5:00 PM
                       CONSULT -
                       Heparin ordered

                       May 9

 56.000 •

 38.000 •

                       May 13

                       12:00 PM
                       Ischemia of
                       hands and feet

                       July 6

                       6:00 AM
                       Amputations
                       start

Missed Information and Lost Limbs

The challenge of how to computerize medical records in the United States is a sensitive issue, and the form that these records will take is a matter of concern to every individual.

Consider the case of an 82-year-old man who underwent successful coronary artery bypass grafting at his local hospital. Several days post-op, when he complained of coolness and color changes in his hands and feet, he was seen by the attending cardiologists and then by a consultant in vascular surgery.

A careful review of his blood tests would have suggested an uncommon but well-known complication of the blood thinner Heparin that causes abnormal clotting in blood vessels. The worst thing a doctor can do in that situation is to order more Heparin, but that is precisely what was done. The outcome for this unfortunate patient was a series of amputations.

It may be tempting to conclude that the failure to carefully review the lab tests was an obvious breakdown in protocol—the fault of the medical team—but this would be a *retrospective* analysis. Lawyers representing hospitals will remind juries that "Hindsight is truly 20/20." The only fair way to assess negligence is to apply a *prospective* review of the patient's medical chart. The form of a medical chart, and the ways in which it presents or omits information, has a profound influence on the decisions that follow. In this case, when the patient's chart is presented chronologically in the form of serial data, the flawed decision-making process is self-evident.

Although a medical chart may not be available to practitioners in an electronic format because the hospital's software may be inadequate, the chart will certainly be the centerpiece of any trial that follows a catastrophic outcome.

A flow chart like this, which clearly shows the trend of a patient's blood count before and after May 8, could have alerted caregivers to complications and prevented multiple amputations of the patient's limbs.

BEYOND TECHNOLOGY

This retreat in the Thousand Islands offers safe harbor and a sense of ease.

A narrow view of the challenge of automating business has brought us to the point where billion-dollar enterprise systems languish on tens of thousands of computer desktops because their relevance and purpose are lost on the end users, who know that aside from using this miracle of computer science, they also have a job to do in order to get paid. What's missing is a clear link in the minds of the end users between their own jobs, their effectiveness in those jobs, the success of the company, and that damned new system that promised to "transform" the business.

Over the past two summers my wife and I have shopped for a summer house in the Thousand Islands region of upstate New York, where 1,800 islands float in the St. Lawrence River and for a century and a half have inspired the construction of fantastic summer cottages. Some of these buildings can be described as almost magical in their design. Their size, shape, details, and the way they sit confidently and respectfully just feet above this huge and powerful river simply delight. On one morning we looked at two properties.

The first was a home designed by and built for the architect who had served the Eastman family for years. It was a modest house that sat solidly but comfortably on a granite slope on the corner of an island. It wasn't alone on the island; in fact, it sat close to another house of the same era, but together they looked like old friends watching the river flow by. Each window had a distinct character, and all were bordered by handsome blue shutters. Inside the house a small brass crank in the corner of each window allowed for the effortless closure of the shutters—heavy slabs of wood that must have weighed a hundred pounds or more hanging from hinges, high above the river. Kitchen drawers were designed to gently roll closed if left open, and bedrooms were sited so that views and breezes were in abundance for the summertime residents. This house had gracefully stood for a hundred years or so, and still was a pleasure to be within and about. Mechanisms still worked and structures were clearly solid, yet what we noticed about being in this house was our feeling of comfort and closeness to the river.

The second house we viewed that day was of comparable size to the first and on its own island of about one acre. It squatted in the near center of the island—likely a practical decision—equally far from the water on all sides, just to be safe. Inside we found a clean and carefully maintained residence, a solid house no doubt, newer than the first by maybe 60 years. The owner of this property was an engineer who had built the place and had enhanced it over his years of ownership. What was remarkable about this house was that it was clearly an incredibly solid structure. Rooms were of the correct number and very logically organized. Doors and windows were tight-fitting and solid. It seemed that there was nothing not to like about this house. Somehow, though, despite all the technical correctness of this house, I could find little to like. The house was too tightly sealed. Even with a window or two open, the place felt closed. The river seemed so far from the rooms' interiors that it was easy to forget we were on an island.

Somehow this house had been so painstakingly engineered that its creator had lost sight of its purpose—to shelter people who wanted to experience life on an island in the middle of one of North America's largest rivers. What it had become was a monument to man's ability to insulate himself from the elements, to survive the river rather than live with it. That was it: I could survive in this house, but I couldn't live there. The first house sold that summer. Two years later, the second house remains for sale.

Like that second house that my wife and I visited, software systems that are meant to support the very existence of business organizations have been engineered to fulfill the functions necessary for the survival of those organizations—efficient, effective survival—without a care for the needs of the human center of all of these engineering feats.

The software industry has bought and built millions of lines of code that support every imaginable business function. From sales to manufacturing, accounting, planning, and strategy, every square inch of an organization has been addressed by the wonders of computing technology and its automation. All of these solutions are created according to an understanding of the business. This understanding is typically the plan of best practices for how specific disciplines within an organization function, how they interact with each other, and how they collectively comprise the overall corporate operation. All of these definitions are framed by a celebration of the latest technology platform—its stability, scalability, speed, and flexibility. So why is so much of this elegant, powerful technological capability such a difficult pill to swallow for an organization? It's because these are engineered solutions, not designed solutions.

What professional doesn't want to do the best job possible with the tools that are available? Let's assume that the vast majority of workers would like to be part of a wildly successful company and share in the success of that organization. Business technology promises to deliver on this model—enabling these individuals to perform at unprecedented heights of effectiveness and in doing so propel the organization itself to new heights. But in most business systems, something is getting in the way of bringing this vision to fruition. To date, engineering has stood alone, with business as supporting contributor. Rarely do we see design participating in, let along leading, the creation of these objects.

From its shutters to its signage, this house is built to suit its context.

Resting on a rock beside a mighty river, this house is engineered to stand on a firm foundation and designed to offer a warm welcome.

We need to look beyond technology. Technical platforms and architectures are indeed critically important to the success of any software application, and to discount these would be to suggest that we could purchase a home without asking about the makeup of the plumbing or the integrity of the foundation: *Does the house have brass plumbing or copper? Is the foundation a patchwork of 200-year-old local stones or modern masonry innovations that support the building but also repel groundwater?*

Underperforming business systems and software generally reflect a lack of appreciation for opportunities with the human audience that lie just beyond clean business logic and engineering technology. To create a robust environment where workers not only can survive, but can actually thrive, requires that a complete knowledge of business needs and an understanding of human audiences must equally influence the engineering logic that defines a system.

That house with the blue shutters perched on a rock in the St. Lawrence would be a folly, if it lasted at all, had its engineering and materials not been precisely calculated. However, it represents an outcome that transcends its makeup because it's the product of design considerations that reach beyond technology.

MEANINGFUL INFORMATION

Actionable information is to data access what a Rolex is to 150 grams of gold. There's no denying the value of the raw material, but it's a long way from the potential value and quality of experience that could be realized when it's shaped by a designer.

A well-designed tool is a pleasure to use, even in the most mundane task. Business systems that perform efficiently and gracefully— ones that speak our language, organize data and features just as we need them, seem to anticipate our expectations, and even make us look good—these are the tools that business needs.

The software industry has done a pretty good job at defining what business needs from technology: vast systems providing access to a deep and broad inventory of data; functions and features representing work processes and methods designed for maximum efficiency; and scalability that allows these systems to grow and expand. What business now needs is real and effective human access to all of this capability, for without it we're not much better off for all of these strengths and innovations.

Real and effective human access will not be achieved through larger budgets for so-called change management and more comprehensive training programs. Business needs less systems training, more immediate and effective user adoption, and authentic excitement from a workforce energized by tools that make these people more effective, more efficient, and more capable of performing at the individual level and in turn at the organizational level. This happens only when the human context of the business process is understood.

Understanding business processes beyond the efficient sequenced access to data and execution of functions is a challenge. Data and functions are handy, tidy components with which to organize a system. Unfortunately, they are too limited a tool set for designing a system. But because systems are defined primarily by business stakeholders (people with an intimate understanding of a business's behaviors, decisions, and information needs) and technologists (individuals with a deep understanding of how to define behaviors, functions, and data within a computer), there is little opportunity to define what a business needs from a system beyond these elements.

A data array of numbers and letters is a collection of facts about the operation and performance of an organization. How to translate that data into a form that conveys to a group of individuals all of the messages within that data is a question that should be asked well before consideration of any technology platform or computer code. "Decision support" is one of the oldest descriptors of the benefits that business systems offer, and the term precisely illuminates one of the shortcomings of current tools. Human beings need to see and understand the messages embedded in the data in order to be able to make appropriate responses that advance the organization's goals.

Every executive in the market for software is seeking better performance—to speed up routine tasks, improve overall processes, manage costs, and to increase margins, revenue, and market share. With comprehensive descriptions of the newest technological capabilities, software vendors draw parallels between these performance needs and the capabilities of their wares. For example, it's easy to claim that if employees who must keep time-entry records could more easily record when they work and what tasks they perform throughout the day, their employers will save money, increase the accuracy of performance measures, and improve their chances of success. For one UK company, the simple task of time entry became such a painful task for its thousands of employees that the company instituted a policy that time entry be performed at a certain time on a certain day. That way, managers hoped, employees wouldn't be squeezing the difficult task in between their usual work and perhaps would enter more accurate data.

Like a thousand small pebbles in a thousand shoes of their employees, systems like these slow the workflow at the point where technological capability reaches the desktop and is touched by human users. Rather than setting a goal of fewer stumbling points and more exacting training requirements, business needs an interface to its enterprise system that sparks excitement in its target community of human users—excitement that their work is easier and more enjoyable, that they have become more effective, and that their employer is supplying tools that make them feel like part of a winning team. Training programs that improve individual performance are excellent, but training programs that teach humans how to be productive despite the design flaws of a system are counterproductive. Recognizing the difference leads to success and opportunity.

Of course, the true measure of a system's performance isn't its raw power, but its efficiency and effectiveness. When a system is described as "efficient" or "effective," it's important to understand how these characteristics were measured. For example, when describing computing technologies that drive the back end of a business system, efficiency may be of the highest order. Transaction processing may be honed to the fraction of a millisecond, and the database architecture may be truly superior. But if the human user's experience in navigating the environment and deciphering the language on-screen is difficult and frustrating, that powerful system may be the most inefficient and ineffective machine you deploy in your workplace. When asked about these issues, systems salespeople often begin to describe a rollout sequence that includes those considerable change management and training programs— and their considerable budgets. Delivering technical efficiency and effectiveness isn't enough. The business needs efficiency and effectiveness from the hands and minds of its workforce.

Every business also needs the confidence and faith of its employees, and all managers want to earn the respect and confidence of their staffs. When considering tools to support the development of these important organizational needs, an electronic enterprise system may not be the first thing that comes to mind. Indeed, employee confidence may be the only thing business system manufacturers aren't promising to transform within the organization. Yet deployment of a new system may have a profound impact on the organization's internal brand. Within the mind of every member of the corporation is an impression of the company—its values, its products, and its people. Is this organization smart, caring, and innovative, or is it an organization with conservative values and plodding methods? Like the impressions we carry in our minds of people we've just met and people we've known for a lifetime, employees also form impressions of their employers.

I've met dozens of physicians who have expressed disgust with the systems they are required to use at their respective hospitals. One doctor rolled her eyes as she described the scenario of ordering blood, and told how she sends a human runner to the blood bank rather than interact with a computer system that is too slow. Technically, the system could get the request to the bank at lightning speed. The unfortunate reality is that the system made it difficult to transmit that request in an acceptable amount of time. When the physician described the scenario to me, she made a number of disparaging comments about the decision makers who buy and deploy these systems, saying that "they don't understand what we really need" and that "they're out of touch."

A system that unnecessarily challenges employees will damage the employees' opinion of their employer, or at least the reputation of the managers who decided to deploy such a tool. It's said that a shoddy craftsman blames his tools. But when the tools are unresponsive, confusing, and outright difficult to use, the craftsman may be justified in blaming not only the tools, but also the provider of the tools—the organization. A brand impression begins at home, within the organization, and an inferior tool can adversely impact one of an organization's most valuable assets.

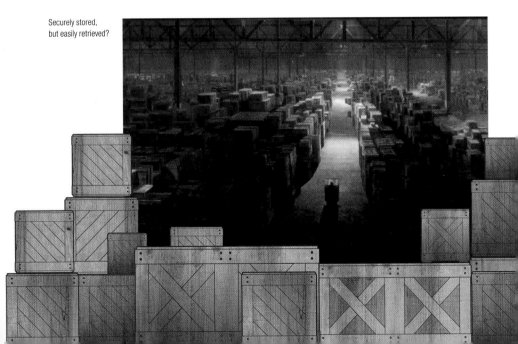

Securely stored,
but easily retrieved?

A Shortcut through the Warehouse

Muscular data-warehousing technology can provide a single access to information in every area of a business operation and can churn out invaluable reports on how the business is operating. But when a data warehouse is difficult to navigate, the search to retrieve a precious bit of information can seem as daunting as locating the Ark of the Covenant in the dimly lit warehouse depicted in the final scene of *Raiders of the Lost Ark*.

Like many global corporations, Rohm and Haas, which manufactures chemicals and other specialty materials, has long relied on a data-warehousing system from SAP to manage all its information assets. Thousands of the company's managers and other employees use the system to mine data throughout the company about its research and development, manufacturing, purchasing, inventory, marketing, and sales, and to generate reports based on these data.

Several years ago, company executives realized that their managers needed better tools to find the reports they needed. Rohm and Haas asked my company to see how the usability of the system could be improved without compromising the integrity of the software, its warranty, or its compatibility with upgrades.

When we sent a designer, a human factors expert, and a technologist to interview managers at their desks and watch them perform specific tasks, we discovered an area that could be improved. The managers knew exactly what information they wanted, but they didn't know how to ask for it. For example, if you wanted a report on this month's production in Singapore, you would first need to confirm that such a report existed. To do this, you would have to search a stand-alone help system, using *exactly the right acronym and prefix.* Once you found that term—which wasn't easy, because the reports weren't organized by subject—you would have to return to the reporting tool within the business warehouse to request the report. Even then, you might not be able to obtain it. Sometimes, after much frustration, managers succeeded in locating a report and processing a request only to be confronted by an error message announcing that their job titles didn't permit them to view it without requesting authorization.

Obtaining information from the data warehouse was so cumbersome that the company was making a significant investment in staffing its internal help desk.

Some managers didn't even try to use the system. They would ask an assistant to describe what they needed to one of the company's technologists, who would then enter a query into the system and run the report. The assistant would come back to the manager 24 or 48 hours later and ask, "Is this what you're looking for?" And often the manager would say, "Well, almost"—and a back-and-forth process would ensue.

It was clear that the managers needed to be closer to the data, but there were two obstacles: navigation and language.

Our solution was to change what people saw on the screen by creating a new interface—essentially a visitors' center attached to the data warehouse—with directories that enable employees to search a centralized repository of reports and descriptions of reports grouped by subject. They can then request reports, bookmark their favorites, see at a glance whether they have access to certain data, and request permission to review information from other departments, all without toggling back and forth between two systems. Managers and other employees interact directly with this application, which in turn provides the most direct route to information within the data warehouse.

Because this new interface is separate from the data warehouse, it won't be affected as the warehouse is expanded and upgraded. The warehouse doesn't even "know" that the application has been added. The only thing that has changed is that now it has become much easier to find the treasure that lies waiting in the warehouse.

For this interface, design partnered with engineering to provide fast access to a wealth of information.

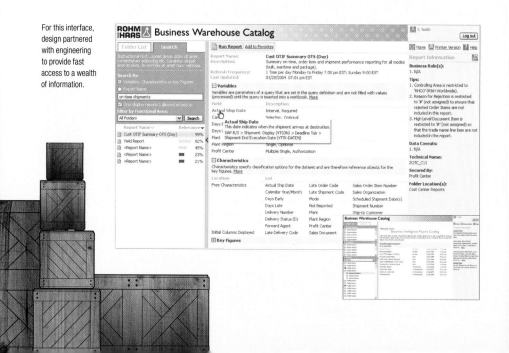

A COMMON LANGUAGE

Baseball players, oenophiles, jazz musicians, broadcast journalists, business analysts, and every other group of individuals who share a common interest have their own language, a discrete set of nouns and verbs that have a unique meaning when used within this group and may rarely be used beyond the group's borders.

The software industry is infamous for its jargon: Login, reboot, drive, merge, debug, failure, and a host of other terms have specific meanings within this community. Layer over this the geographic or culturally specific meanings that we assign to symbols, colors, and even numbers, and there is tremendous opportunity, and tremendous risk, when we begin to create business systems based on language.

A shared business language may be so firmly fixed by the force of habit that it can be very difficult to change. The teaching hospital of an American university recently deployed a new pharmacy system to transmit and fulfill drug orders throughout the hospital. This new system did not accept measurements of drugs in the same increments that had been the tradition within that institution. Although the discrepancy was recognized before the system was deployed, it was considered a training issue and allowed to persist. What was viewed at the launch of this product as a training issue quickly became an urgent safety issue as users across the spectrum of caregivers failed time and again to notice the system's new increments of measurement and repeatedly entered doses of medication in values corresponding to the hospital's previous measures.

Language is not a business tool that we want to leave to chance—or to the whims of our development teams. Words and phrases on the screen will guide an audience, empowering them with access to all the capabilities a system has to offer, or cripple them by forcing them to clumsily move through a trial-and-error process, guessing at the meanings of terms and the results their actions will have.

Hobos and Hieroglyphs

Every business community needs a system that understands its users and speaks their language.

While I was working with IBM in the early 1990s, designing icons, I was acutely aware of the multicultural implications of the small pictographs we were creating. Body parts were too controversial; a simple image of a human hand, no matter what position it took, seemed to conjure up insults and profanity in one country or another (ahh, human beings—we have no shortage of hand gestures for insulting one another!). Human faces were problematic, because aside from needing to represent an appropriate cross section of races, they always looked like severed heads—an uncomfortable image in all cultures. Icons that represented complex actions or represented a group of related objects couldn't be arranged in a series to read from left to right because not all languages read this way. So I became a proponent of the wonderful 26-character icon set we have in the form of the Roman alphabet.

For centuries the alphabet has conveyed the simplest and most complex thoughts between individuals and across vast populations. These symbols, arranged in appropriate combinations, communicate clearly and effectively. Yet our present business environment is a toolbar-crazy world that continues to believe that software is much easier to use if functions buried within pull-down menu systems are presented to users as abstract images on buttons at the top of a screen. Sometimes these images are very bizarre; try to imagine the button icon in a medical system that means "order a blood test."

At IBM we watched our symbolic language carefully, and often we found that words were clearer than any graphic abstraction. In most business systems, cumbersome menu hierarchies are supplied to provide full access to system capabilities. But when toolbar graphics are the remedy, know that the risks for miscommunication and delays will double.

Overuse of iconography suggests an attempt to compensate for an overly complex or disorganized user environment. And remember that no matter how attractive these icons are, each one requires users to understand and retain its associated meaning as well as the result they can expect from selecting the symbol. In this respect, overestimating the abilities of the end users is dangerous and can undermine acceptance of the system. When a product demonstrator says, "Just click a toolbar button," beware. There's no "just" to it.

A	А	
B	Б	
C	В	
D	Г	
E	Д	
F	Е	
G	Ж	
H	З	
I	И	
J	К	
K	Л	
L	М	
M	Н	
N	О	
O	П	
P	Р	
Q	С	
R	Т	
S	У	
T	Ф	
U	Х	
V	Ч	
W	Ш	
X	Э	
Y	Ю	
Z	Я	

AN ACCURATE TRANSLATION

If you want to improve a business system, it would seem logical to talk to the people who use that system on a daily basis.

Experts have been telling the technology industry for years that better outcomes will result when end users participate in the design of business systems. For the most part, this has happened through standard techniques such as surveys, questionnaires, focus groups, and working sessions that ask users to describe what they do and how they believe things should work. These are well-intentioned activities, but results are mixed and usually seriously flawed.

People really do like to influence the design of a tool that will be a large part of their day and will have a powerful influence on their effectiveness in their jobs. Unfortunately, these inputs are too often taken as gospel and used to define a set of design criteria that are not the best guidelines for constructing a system. These audiences are just not capable of providing design direction. They're too close to existing tools and methods and don't have the skills to design a software system, even when that system's sole purpose is to support their work.

If people can't tell you what they need, how can you find out? They can show you.

A generation ago, a Japanese auto manufacturer decided to build a line of luxury sedans for the U.S. market. The leadership of Toyota understood the technology of the automobile, so almost anything was technically possible, and they also knew that they would not be able to compete against BMW and Mercedes-Benz, or even Honda's Acura and Nissan's Infiniti, unless their product offered the consumer a design that exceeded what was already available. But where to find the direction for this new design?

Rather than relying solely on survey data and focus groups, the design of these new luxury cars would be inspired by the firsthand experience of designers and researchers living as members of the target user community—understanding their day-to-day routines and discovering what this new car could be in order to transcend what was known. Members of Toyota's design team moved into Laguna Beach, California. They loaded their groceries into the trunks of their cars, picked up dry cleaning, and hung out at country clubs. In order to discover the advantages their product could bring to the marketplace, they witnessed the entire context in which the target user community existed, down to watching how women with fancy manicures managed a steering wheel. This product manufacturer worked tirelessly to understand its customers' true user requirements, and in 1989, when Toyota introduced the Lexus LS 400, it brought a very appealing product to the marketplace and raised the bar for an industry.

The success of Lexus did not come because Toyota's leaders asked their potential customers to design the car with them; they clearly understood that focus groups and surveys would not be the source of revolutionary design ideas. The company relied on the design process as an exercise in observing and interpreting some of the ways in which people interact with its product, and they didn't send just anyone into the field to design the research process and execute the analysis. Skilled designers and design researchers performed this work, and their findings set the direction for innovation. The result was a new product that felt as luxurious as it looked.

BEAUTIFUL DATA

Too often—in fact, most of the time—well-designed software is thought to be software that is visually appealing: cleanly designed forms, consistent and purposeful application of colors and fonts, slick buttons, and neat animations that slide menus open and expand and contract directory structures. To think of these aesthetic treatments as genuine design advances is like putting lipstick on the proverbial pig.

Not long ago I was amazed to discover that a well-known system that has the reputation of being one of the most notoriously hard to use enterprise systems on the market boasted of having a user interface designed by one of the world's most famous design firms. It seemed implausible, but when I visited that design firm's web site, I saw that it was true. A page described how the company had designed the user interface of the enterprise system. On closer examination, what was described was the design firm's involvement in choosing the color palette, drawing sets of tab controls, buttons, and icons, and formatting the display characteristics. This is not user interface design. This is the simplest form of graphic design, a cosmetic makeover within an electronic display. Unless the designer is concerned with the sequencing of these controls, the language of the user interface, the navigation of the environ-ment, and the ability of the user to learn and adopt the tool quickly and effectively, little more has been done than to supply handsome graphics and perhaps descriptions for their continued use.

The software developer that commissioned that design for its enter-prise system undoubtedly made the investment with high hopes, but there may have been a basic misunderstanding about what would be delivered: an appealing graphic design or an appealing user interface design that would make the system's remarkable technology more accessible.

The look and feel of technology is commonly confused with its usability. The look of a display is important, but it represents just a small fraction of a system's design, and elaborate graphics can even interfere with the messages. We don't need business systems with prettier palettes; we need systems that reflect an understanding of the business and a projection of that business in a way that is easily accessible to everyone who uses the system.

Good design supports and enhances the functions of a product, but decoration, no matter how skillfully executed, is superficial. That house in the center of an island in the St. Lawrence is not going to change its nature by artfully filling its rooms with moose heads, mounted fish, and antique snowshoes and fishing poles. It is fundamentally flawed as a design, and its very essence needs to be reconsidered as an object whose purpose is not only to satisfy the need for shelter but also to provide a desirable experience. So it is with a business system, which brings success to an organization only when it satisfies the men and women who are striving to be successful as individuals.

WHAT BUSINESS HASN'T EVEN THOUGHT OF

Rethinking business, shifting paradigms, thinking outside the box —countless business books have made innumerable suggestions for how to innovate and move your company "to the next level." But the typical techniques of software development, systems evaluation, and purchase simply don't allow for exploration of forms that challenge convention and may possibly hold the key to true transformation and human effectiveness inside a newly invented business.

The design process provides business with an opportunity to invent and refine concepts in order to figure out exactly what is needed, to explore alternatives, and then to define a form that meets that need most effectively. When done well, this process provides opportunity for innovation and excitement that can invigorate a business and produce a revolutionary and genuinely innovative outcome.

Consider the construction of an opera house or the galleries of an art museum. The basic functional needs that these two buildings must meet could drive their creation in the direction of a safe and effective, if perhaps boring, four walls and roof. Their size will be dictated by a requirement to reflect a specific performance configuration or to house a collection of art of a certain size. To answer this challenge with specifications based only on engineering knowhow and an inventory of the facts concerning the performances and

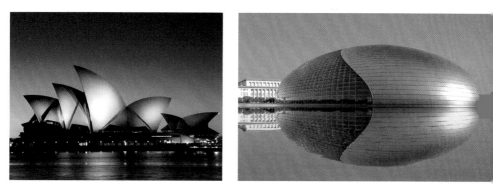

artwork (their numbers, sizes, and their anticipated audiences) will likely result in an uninspired and perhaps uninviting outcome. Of course, this isn't what happens in real life.

Museum leaders and performing arts executives in Sydney, Beijing, and many other cities realize that their investment in the building to house the treasures of their business is in itself an opportunity to draw crowds, to enhance the human experience with the art, and to reinforce their brands by becoming as memorable an impression in the collective mind of their audience as any painting or moment of action on the stage. A surge of innovative, imaginative architecture over the past 20 years is a terrific record of this.

Powerful brands— The innovative design and engineering of the Sydney Opera House (left) and China's National Centre for the Performing Arts in Beijing (right), are symbols of national pride. (Architects: Jorn Utzon; Paul Andreu)

Massive columns support ceilings, frame paintings, and transport visitors within the Sainsbury Wing. (Architects: Venturi Scott Brown and Associates)

Approach the Sainsbury Wing of the National Gallery on London's Trafalgar Square, and what you see is as dramatic as a stage set—a work of classical architecture punctuated by glass geometries revealing light and life within as well as darkened recesses like the spaces at the edges of the backdrops on a stage, framing the scene of the play, all hinting at the treasures and experiences the building holds. Enter the building and you'll find stone arches and columns, corridors of linked rooms, and vast walls that seem to exist only in the service of framing the masterpieces among them, allowing you to see the faces of saints and the palettes of master painters from yards away as they gently draw you closer and closer. The design of this building is the visual equivalent of a listening device that allows us to hear a sound at a greater distance than our ears allow, and in this case to hear certain notes or chords being struck in carefully measured sequence.

Perhaps it may seem a bit grandiose to link landmark architecture to business systems or to draw parallels between an organization's data and the artistic treasures of a museum. But just consider the price of business systems—in the hundreds of millions of dollars in some cases—and consider the value of the data assets held by a company. Yet when we build business systems, too often we settle for building roofs and walls and stacking up the data—safe and dry, but hardly an ideal arrangement for human access. We can do so much better. Systems development gives us an opportunity to understand what the human experience needs to be, to imagine what it might be, and to invent a great experience.

When employees and management have been working in certain ways over a long period, it's unrealistic to expect thinking that reaches far beyond what these individuals have known; they know what they know. The design process affords an opportunity to explore alternatives to the known, to measure the validity of these options, and to allow business leaders to see alternatives they may never have considered.

When the Prince of Wales saw an early design for the Sainsbury Wing, he pronounced it "a monstrous carbuncle on the face of a much-loved and elegant friend." He was only looking at a model of a proposed design—no damage had been done, and other designs could be explored. And so they were, and what we have today is a masterpiece to house masterpieces.

Classical details echo neighboring buildings; geometry heralds the new.

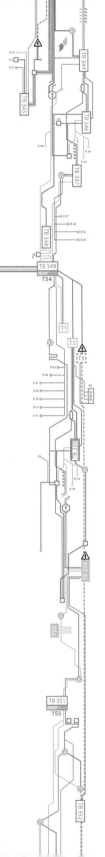

Channeling Rivers of Energy

One of the biggest business headaches of the twenty-first century is data overload. New technologies continually make available more data, but what business really needs is better information.

In the business of managing the supply of energy, the need for strong decision support is a critical requirement. The task of channeling the flow of energy around the world has become increasingly consolidated among global companies such as E.ON, which coordinates energy across Europe, and the National Grid, which owns the electricity network throughout most of the United Kingdom and also distributes power to millions of Americans in New England. The urgent need to quickly and accurately interpret massive quantities of volatile data is stimulating these companies to find new ways to convert data into information.

In my home state of Pennsylvania, the electric power grid is managed by a regional transmission organization, PJM Interconnection, which serves 51 million persons in 13 states. At the company's headquarters in Valley Forge, a generation dispatcher is on duty 24/7 to monitor and modulate the supply of power minute by minute, sometimes reconfiguring those supplies to avoid overloading utility lines when demand peaks.

On two walls of PJM's control room are video displays, one about 30 feet wide and 15 feet high, and another measuring about 70 by 15 feet. One is a giant dashboard that shows the overall load of the grid and the current balance between supply and demand; the other is a geographic map showing rivers of electricity pouring out of more than a thousand sources large and small, from nuclear reactors to windmill farms. The generation dispatcher also has six desktop monitors that display projections and spreadsheet data about supply and demand, prices, and weather. While comparing real-time data to the computer's daily projections, the dispatcher uses three keyboards to construct new projections and make decisions. Any unexpected problem—a shutdown along the supply line or a sudden surge in demand—means that the dispatcher must calculate and initiate a solution within as little as two minutes.

Several seasons ago, as PJM's executives considered replacing older technologies with new systems, they realized that there were opportunities beyond technical architectures and platforms. It seemed clear that PJM's professionals were working minute by minute with information that was not optimally displayed. The company asked Electronic Ink for advice about how to give the dispatchers more information without increasing their mental load. Designers and researchers then led a process to gain insight into how the data could be presented more effectively.

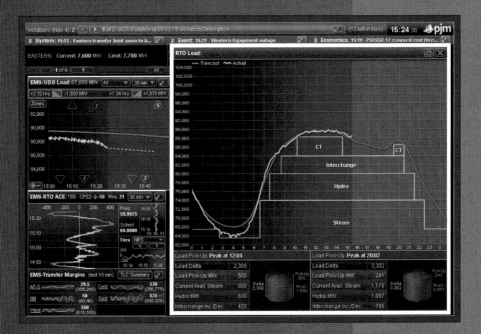

At PJM, dashboard display cells (top) provide at-a-glance views of conditions on the electric power grid across 13 states.
Data visualizations (above) translate tabular data into trend lines that show relationships among the data.

When a design team observed dispatchers at work, they saw that they were continuously consulting more than a dozen sources of tabular data in order to form a mental picture of emerging trends. The solution was to design a shortcut.

Visual alternatives to the spreadsheet format were drafted, tested, and refined to be compatible with the high-pressure work environment of the dispatchers as well as the technical platform that would support them. The result was a new dashboard that fuses and translates data into trend lines, graphs, and other dynamic visual information, summarizing and supplementing the spreadsheet data to allow dispatchers to spot anomalies more quickly and manage by exception.

If the development process had been limited to finding a technological answer to what the business felt was needed and what the dispatchers said they wanted, the outcome would have been much different. A new dashboard probably isn't something the dispatchers would have requested, nor are technologists well equipped to shape content into forms that people can easily comprehend. But by reconsidering the array of data through a design process that analyzed the minute-by-minute tasks of the dispatchers, it was transformed.

SEVEN
BELIEVE IT WHEN YOU SEE IT

I'll never forget the first time I saw a workshop filled with proto-types of new products.

During my first semester of college, I was given an informal tour of the industrial design modeling shop at Carnegie Mellon University. In the subbasement of an academic building was a huge room lined with table saws, band saws, planers, sanders, and drill presses. Next to the shop were a painting booth and a room for assembling con-structions. What I would see created in this space over the next few months amazed me; industrial design students were using wood and foam to build beautiful models of toys, kitchen appliances, table lamps, and other products.

In my eyes, these objects were beautiful not because I agreed with every aesthetic choice the designers had made, but because they looked so real—they allowed me to understand their shapes, colors, and textures, and to imagine myself using them. A model of a toy had brightly colored surfaces that looked just like the plastic material that was proposed for the toy, and I could understand how the parts of the toy fit together and how a child might play with it. All of this information was available to me through a model—a carefully constructed but cheap and flimsy version of the proposed design.

These models weren't used to specify fabrication of the finished products. In product design, the purpose of a model is to transform pages of written specifications and two-dimensional sketches into a three-dimensional object so that designer, marketer, manufacturer, and consumer can reach a consensus on a common vision—quickly, accurately, and, most importantly, affordably. I saw that once a model had served that purpose, it would be relegated to a corner of some designer's desk for a while and eventually tossed in the trash.

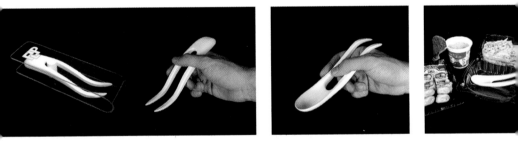

What if? Imagine a reusable utensil that's both a fork and a spoon, one that's easy to clean and store in a desk. This prototype lets everyone envision the same tool.

An industrial designer who models the interior of a new automobile and an architect who constructs a scale model of a building are doing the same thing. Each provides a necessarily diverse audience of professionals who participate in a product's development with a cost-effective, meaningful method of evaluating a design well in advance of its production, at a stage when revisions, updates, and other options can still be explored. But in software development, something very different happens. Because designers and their modeling abilities are not typically resident within the software development process, developers are left to create prototypes. The outcome isn't nearly as successful. Developers move to the materials they know—code—and begin to generate working models. The shock of my first experience with this situation early in my career is still vivid.

WHEN PROTOTYPE BECOMES PRODUCT

In 1990, when I was working in IBM's software development lab at Warwick, I found myself regarded as the guy who was expected to improve the look and the feel of the applications that were under development. I immediately found myself inserted *in medias res*: in the middle of things.

With all the optimism and enthusiasm of a newly minted designer, I immediately asked to see a prototype of one of the applications so that I could assess the design of the displays and the way in which a user was expected to interact with it. What I saw in the prototype was a lot of opportunity to reduce the number of displays, improve their flow, and clarify the manner in which information was displayed, and I said as much to the developers. The response I received from these men was a cold stare—a mixture of utter amazement at my

This prototype shows everyone how a new form will perform all its functions—how smoothly it pours, how its lid lifts off, and how it sounds when it whistles.

ignorance and disgust at my presumption to speak so out of turn. I had no idea that in this new world of software development, prototypes weren't the throwaway, temporary tools made by designers.

In software development, the prototype likely becomes the product's prerelease version, and subsequently becomes the product itself. Software is given form on the screen of a computer through a process driven by technical architecture and engineering of the back end. Software prototypes are the engineer's expression of documented requirements, and the materials being manipulated—working computer code—are as costly and rigid as sheet metal on an automobile assembly line.

Typically, because software prototypes are composed of such dear materials and painstakingly programmed to perform in a certain manner, the die has been cast before anyone outside the development environment is allowed to see the software, let alone test it in the hands of the product's end users. This method completely defies logic. It reduces opportunity for exploration and discovery, affords no chance to measure the displays for user acceptance, and it is an enormously expensive and risky way to work.

When skilled designers and their methods are missing from the first stage of the development process, there is little opportunity to explore the possibilities of how the software could most effectively take form on the user's screen until a significant amount of money and time has been committed. And when prototypes become product without giving nontechnical stakeholders an opportunity to see the software until it's too late to make changes, the finished product may be ill suited to its purpose or even useless.

The software industry has tried to improve the development process by dividing it into ever smaller steps, breaking up the long sequences of documentation and code generation in the waterfall method into incremental cycles and calling the development process "rapid," "agile," "extreme," "spiral," or "scrum." But reorganizing and renaming the same old methodology won't solve the problem, because technology doesn't have the tools to match a product to its audience. For business software to become satisfying and cost-effective, its development cycle must include designers and the design process from the outset.

ENVISIONING THE CHRYSLER BUILDING

Look at any skyline, and you will see buildings that once existed only in the minds of the architects who imagined them.

In 1928, how did architect William Van Alen persuade automobile manufacturer Walter P. Chrysler to build a gleaming tower of steel, bricks, and glass that would project to the world the success, power, and ingenuity of a company and its people? First, never underestimate the power of appealing to the ego in the executive suite. Having an architect who is game to build the world's tallest structure doesn't hurt, either. But to transform such a grand ambition into reality, it was necessary for the founder's business goals and the designer's ideas to come together to form a common vision, and for this vision to be further refined by engineers who understood every aspect of the building's structure and systems. A business titan, a visionary architect, and engineers asked to construct a structure like no other before it—this could be a recipe for disaster. But skylines prove it can be done.

Our aspirations for the software that runs our business operations should be no less lofty than those of the tycoons whose buildings define our city skylines: a high standard of solidly constructed, reliably efficient, and technically innovative structures that are visually appealing and as imaginative as they are practical. To achieve this result, architects make sketches and build models of the possibilities for their clients, engineers, and zoning officials to review. In contrast, the software development process focuses on the written word—lengthy descriptions of what is wanted from a system, descriptions that become a set of requirements explaining what the technology must do. This process keeps the focus of software systems on engineering, their essence defined by their computing power and technical sophistication rather than their relationship to human users and their ability to project to this audience a sense of empowerment, trust, and even delight. How people will see and touch the features of a new software product is typically a question that is left to be addressed only after the developers solve the engineering challenge.

Beyond words— Imagine trying to construct the Chrysler Building from prose-based specifications without using blueprints or drawings.

What does a software application look like? How is it structured? If you ask technologists these questions, they will describe data structures, layers, and interfaces between the layers and their components. But from the user's perspective, what does the software look like?

Unfortunately, what the users see on the screen is very often a result of careful consideration given to every aspect of the system *except* for them. What users are faced with is a product whose form has been dictated by engineering strategy and specifications for inventories of data and features. This lack of consideration for the human factor manifests itself in user interfaces that are little more than an afterthought to the challenges of coding.

From my earliest experiences with software development I've been amazed to see software teams move through a development cycle without creating a shared vision of how the end product will look on the screen. Perhaps what is even more amazing is that budgets are drawn up and checks are approved by business executives who are agreeing to commit precious funds to something they haven't seen and don't completely understand.

If we can see a prototype of a product before it's built, we can see how it will work. Making prototypes is the technique that designers use to spark love affairs between consumers and their favorite products. But before anyone can feel the love, everyone involved in a product's creation needs to be able to explore the possibilities—without blowing the budget.

A prototype can take many forms. Sometimes even a sketch on a napkin is enough to suggest the form of an idea or a concept and elicit reactions from an audience, reactions that drive further refinement of the idea or confirm the appropriateness of the form. A prototype also may be a full-scale model, or a set of blueprints.

Blueprints are pictures that allow us to visualize the future; in plan form, an aerial view of a floor, they allow us to imagine walking from room to room and to predict the experience we will have living and working in a space. In section form, diagrams that allow us to understand vertical elements in the design within a space, we can see staircases, doorways, windows, baseboards, and crown moldings. If we choose, we can page through a set of blueprints to see how the plumbing will carry water and waste to and from the kitchen and bathrooms and how the electrical system will be arranged.

What all true prototypes have in common is their fleeting nature. Their sole purpose is to facilitate communication among diverse audiences, elicit their reactions, and drive further design enhancement. A prototype is meant to be thrown away: No one will ever live

Prototypes made with ink on paper are spontaneous, inexpensive, and invaluable for exploring and articulating ideas.

in it, drive it, or use it for any other purpose. However inexpensive and ephemeral it may be, a prototype allows us to imagine the possibilities, explore options, and examine wild notions without the limitations of cost, time, or physics. Most importantly, a prototype allows individuals to understand a proposed design and for groups to share this understanding.

When we see a prototype, we can imagine what might be—bringing a creative, idealistic vision incrementally back to earth as we evaluate it against the realities of its construction requirements and seek fabrication techniques that rise to the challenge.

THE HIDDEN COSTS OF GUESSWORK

When the prototyping techniques of the traditional design process are absent, the software development cycle poses three significant risks: accuracy, innovation, and cost. Few things are more important to any business initiative than these three elements. But whenever software prototypes are used only to prove the stability of the code and to incrementally move an application to delivery, all three elements suffer.

Most software is built according to a requirements document that describes in prose exactly what a software product will do. If our only concern is what the system will do, it may be sufficient to specify the functions that it must perform; for example, a requirement for an electronic medical record may be, *Allow the user to enter the system and retrieve blood pressure data.* But how this will be done is another question altogether. Actually, it's two questions: How will the function be performed by the technical architecture on the back end, and how it will be accomplished by the human being who is responsible for retrieving the data? This is where accuracy is at risk.

The initial requirements for system functions are driven by business specialists who intimately understand the domain where the software will be deployed. These subject-matter experts can provide a complete inventory of things they *want* from a system, but few of them are capable of describing precisely what they *need*. Buyers of medical record systems may know that they want a system that can store blood pressure data and record new measurements, but they don't know what is needed to best accomplish this, from either an engineering standpoint or the perspective of the users. This is where a designer's prototypes are valuable.

Seeing how the data will look and how it will be manipulated on the screen gives technical and nontechnical stakeholders a common understanding of exactly what is being proposed. It also enables them to validate the stated requirement and assess the accuracy of the proposed means of satisfying that requirement by asking, *Does this system do what we want? How easy is it to use?* Modeling the stated requirements in this way at an early stage of the development process mitigates risk—the risk that what is ultimately built will fail to be what's needed for the business because it reflects an incomplete or misguided inventory of what was wanted.

Just as a prototype can be used to increase the accuracy of a software application's specification, it also can maximize the opportunity for innovation. Because technologists own the vast majority of tasks within the software development cycle, innovation is typically seen from the perspective of coding or systems design. But new data structures and coding techniques that are wildly innovative may seem obtuse and clumsy to an end user, and one only needs to look as far as some of the largest and most expensive enterprise systems on the market for examples of these so-called innovative systems. As the manufacturers of these enormous systems moved to exploit Web browser technology to distribute functionality across vast organizations, they touted these new products as fantastically innovative—and indeed they are, from a technical viewpoint. However, even though challenges of technology, software distribution, and performance have been tackled and in many cases brilliantly resolved, only the technology shows real innovation in product design. On-screen, where men

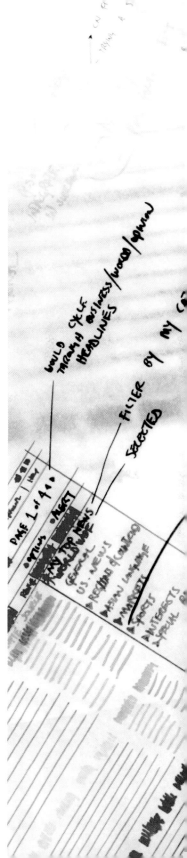

and women must be able to effectively manipulate these tools in order for all of this innovation to be worthwhile, these systems are too often nothing short of abysmal.

When designers use drawings and other inexpensive methods to preview a software application, intense collaboration can happen, new ideas can be encouraged and explored, and genuine innovation can occur. By showing alternative ways to present data to the end users, a designer can lead a product team through an exploration of possibilities within a few hours or even in a matter of minutes. Models can be created and thrown away, and concepts that seem to have merit can be taken to prospective audiences for evaluation, then further refined. With each iteration, technologists can evaluate and advise so that ultimately the finished product will be engineered to reflect a thorough and thoughtful exploration of the possibilities.

These sketches of screen views are prototypes that were created in minutes to review new forms of data presentation, display control, and hierarchies of color.

Ironically, many people who have never used this process assume that it must be expensive—that involving designers and exploring the possibilities through multiple product models will raise the price of the project and delay its schedule. In fact, it's far more costly to order software without fully understanding how it will serve both the business needs and the human needs, and without exploiting the opportunity that any development effort holds for innovation. The cost of not getting it right the first time accumulates steadily in the form of ongoing expenses for training programs and subsequent rereleases—significant costs so common that often they're built into the licensing agreements for large enterprise systems.

Charting a New Course

Often the future turns out to look nothing like what we expected.

A few years ago, a major financial institution decided to commission a replacement for one component of its electronic reporting system. The company's system is a proprietary surveillance tool that automatically gathers data about the trading records of its stockbrokers. This data can be analyzed to confirm that the actions of individual traders are in line with standard patterns of behavior and best practices, or to detect whether certain groups of transactions might signal a pattern of fraud.

The company's business goal, to create a system that could spot patterns of fraud more quickly and more accurately, couldn't have been clearer. The company also had very clear ideas about how the data should be displayed: When we talked with analysts who used the tool, they told us that no graphing capabilities would be necessary. We were puzzled. No graphs for a database that represented a very significant number of trades on a daily basis? But we soon learned why. We discovered that the analysts who used the system had never had access to graphs that properly supported their work, so they were working from spreadsheets to analyze data and convert it to information—a task that computers are ideally suited to perform.

In order to achieve innovation and avoid replicating the present, it's essential to explore alternative concepts, question assumptions, and test prototypes. Over the next few weeks, a team of our designers worked with the company to explore ways of using data visualization techniques (including graphs). The analysts explained what information they needed, the designers proposed new ways to interpret and communicate the data, and the designers and technologists worked together to create low-tech models to test each concept.

The outcome of this teamwork is something that no one expected: an electronic workbench that provides immediate access to high-level trends and the ability to access low-level details from the same source—in a format based entirely on graphs. This innovation never would have been possible without a corporate commitment to reexamine existing methods and to venture beyond the known in collaboration with professional designers, technologists, and its own expert analysts.

New forms of yardsticks can quantify trends.

BREAKING THE CYCLE OF FAILURE

How we go about designing a product will directly impact its quality and its success. This is why so many business systems fall short of expectations once they are in the hands of their users. The process by which they're designed is defective, and the people who design them are not professionally equipped to do the job.

Most business software is the product of teamwork between two groups of professionals. In one corner are the business experts, knowledgeable in how work is done (or should be done). In the other corner are the technologists, ready and able to code almost anything. Rarely does either group include individuals who are trained in the traditional process of product design. By default, by sheer political might, or by chance—depending on the organization—either the business side or the technology side will take ownership of figuring out how the software will look and feel. The ineffective result of this collaboration can be witnessed in the many software development methodologies that have been documented, institutionalized, revised, praised, and condemned, all in the name of building better systems. Yet every one of these methods is pretty much as ineffective as any other when we consider the quality of the user's experience with these tools.

Throughout the 1990s, business and technical experts favored the systems development process called the waterfall method. In this process, business experts compile a complete inventory of all the functional requirements of a system, and then technologists write the specifications for a system that will satisfy the software product's description. These and other prose-based specifications become a thick set of documents that are handed off to a team of developers who begin the long and often painful process of building this large and thoroughly documented system. Like rivers at the headwaters of a waterfall, the streams of code join together, forming a mass whose course becomes increasingly difficult to alter as it cascades toward its terminus. Eventually, after developers have spent months writing hundreds and thousands of lines of code, the business stakeholders who were involved in the early stages of product definition are brought back into the process to see the results of the developers' efforts at a stage called user acceptance testing (UAT). This is where the problems begin to surface.

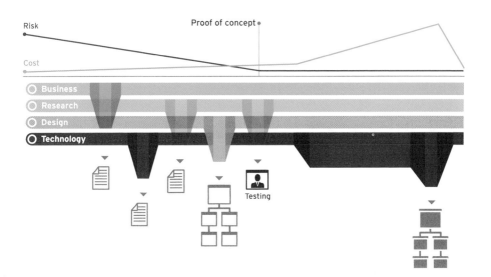

User acceptance testing is possibly the most Orwellian misnomer I have encountered in my career. Typically, no users are asked to participate in this step of the development cycle, and the concern for any level of acceptance by users is marginal at best. Essentially this is a check to ensure that the software code coming out of the development phase can perform every function that was inventoried in the requirement document. For example, *Can this application be used to retrieve blood pressure data?* This is the moment when the business experts obtain their first real view of the software on-screen, and it is among the riskiest junctures in the software development process. Very often, the reaction from the business side is *This isn't what I expected.* Not unreasonably, the technologists respond by saying, *This is what you asked for, but if this isn't what you want, tell us what you need.* At this point all bets are off, and what happens next is anyone's guess.

The beauty of prose is its highly variable nature. When a writer assembles words in combination with one another, the choice of one word over another can shift the meaning of what is being presented to the reader ever so slightly, or possibly quite dramatically. A set of words will paint a unique picture in the mind's eye of every reader; that's why a film version of your favorite novel may look nothing like the book you've imagined. Surely this dynamic is what makes the enjoyment of literature such a personal and immensely popular pastime. Yet this same magic—the ambiguity that allows

When researchers and designers are present, early models of software can be tested with target audiences, and specifications can be refined to support technical implementation.

each of us to visualize something unique in the same set of words—is the worst possible thing that could happen in a product design cycle. When software developers work from written descriptions, it creates havoc.

Business experts and technologists speak somewhat different languages, and as programmers interpret the words describing business requirements, it's unlikely that their vision of the tool they are programming will accurately reflect the tool that the business stakeholders believe they have described. In user acceptance testing, the gap between what the business side had envisioned and what the developers have coded becomes painfully obvious. In the waterfall method, when all of these disconnects emerge toward the end of the development cycle, the next stage is typically a combination of responses: Immediately rework the screen displays if changes can be made without dramatically impacting the software code; devise a training plan to address critical bugs, the glaring issues that can't be fixed but will most definitely trip up users; and make a list of changes to the product's features that need to be reconsidered in subsequent releases. Or even: Rewrite the specifications and repeat the process.

This situation couldn't last. Because in the waterfall method technologists alone had written the code, they took the blame for delivering unacceptable displays and software applications that were impossibly difficult to use. But the technologists had only delivered what they had been asked to code. Enter the "agile" methodologies, and the age of shared guilt.

Partly as an attempt to give the business side an earlier opportunity to see new software products, developers devised new forms of the development cycle—rapid, agile, extreme, spiral, and scrum—in which segments of an application are designed, developed, and reviewed for accuracy as teams begin building the next logical piece of the application. Over time, these pieces come together to form the whole system. No longer are thousands of lines of code in jeopardy during a momentous unveiling of the software application; instead, business stakeholders review a sample that is the result of just weeks, days, or even hours of development. Then, if a developer has not coded the written requirements into a user interface that reflects the thinking of the business stakeholders, the scope of the

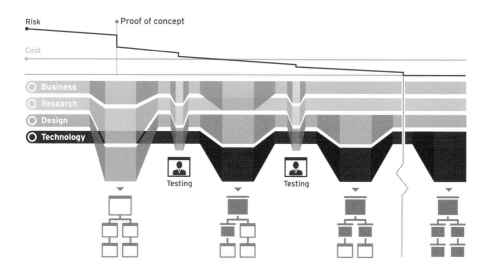

task to rework that code is not tremendously great. Theoretically, over time, a sequence of well-designed segments of the system will be linked into a well-designed whole.

Sound like a reasonable way to solve the problem? It isn't. Unfortunately, a component of the system reviewed at any stage does not represent a picture that is complete enough to make possible an accurate or thorough critical assessment. What evolves is a collection of parts. At this point Victor Frankenstein's monster may come to mind.

Imagine that you are working directly with a contractor to build a new headquarters building for your company. The contractor has been given a highly detailed document—not a set of blueprints—describing the characteristics of the building, from the number of stories and the square footage of each floor to the grade and the color of the carpeting to be installed in the corridors. Early in the project the contractor completes the construction of five steps in the stairway that will serve as the emergency exit from the top to the bottom of the building. He calls you in, points to the paragraph of text in the requirements document describing the stairway, and asks you to sign a release confirming that the five steps are "correct." This would be impossible. You wouldn't be able to see how these steps will physically relate to the other steps that must be built, how they will be placed within the building, and where they will land the workers as they head for the exits.

Design and research bring to the agile development process an early view of the product that can predict the rate of user acceptance and give technologists a clear vision of what's needed.

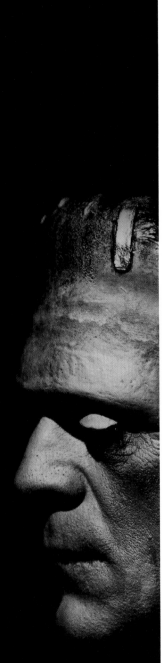

Without a comprehensive model of the user interface, agile or rapid software development is likely to deliver a pieced-together solution.

It's assumed that by delivering smaller pieces of a software application through relatively short bursts of design and development, the rapid methodologies of the development cycle will mitigate the risk of disappointing the business stakeholders and in turn the end users. Although these methods may ease the trepidation of the business side over the grandiose unveiling of a system, what is being delivered is of no higher quality from the perspective of the end users.

These methods do nothing to expand the shared vocabulary of the business and technology professionals who are performing the work, because they do not incorporate design techniques that allow all the members of the team to visualize the software prior to any code development. So instead we see new systems with no substantial improvement in the quality of the end user's experience; but now the failure is not just the fault of the developers. Because the business team has participated in every stage of the process, reviewing incrementally delivered pieces of the system, they too own part of the blame for systems that ultimately disappoint.

An unintended consequence of the agile development method is the fact that business experts, who used to do most of the finger-pointing when systems failed to resonate with users, are less willing to assume this role now that they share more responsibility. In the resulting silence, everyone is left to believe that the problem is solved.

The cycle of disappointment and failure that sabotages our business technology can be broken only by reconfiguring the standard software development process. Although the waterfall and rapid methodologies have proven tremendously effective in developing computer code, they are weak at best for the creation of human-centered tools.

Every standard method of software development lacks flexibility, affordable and effective modeling of the proposed system, and early proof that the system will achieve business goals through effective use. These are the very strengths of design, the arrows in the quiver of every capable designer. Whenever designers contribute design methods to the development process, and whenever human consumers of the end product are effectively guided to participate in the process from start to finish, the development cycle leads to products that return their investment many times over.

LEAVE NOTHING TO INTERPRETATION

No matter what development method technologists use, business stakeholders need an early and accurate view of a proposed system, a preview of how it will work and what it will look like on the screen. Technologists also need to see a proposed display's design in order to confirm its viability within the technology environment. Users, too, need to see the display strategy in order to validate the assumptions that have driven its design.

But what should a prototype for a software system be?

The simplest, most inexpensive prototype is a drawing. A designer can quickly translate the written requirements for a system into pictures—a *product map* that describes the landscape of all system displays and their organization; display-level *wireframes* that articulate navigation controls, access to features and functions, and the presentation of information; and *aesthetic models* that show the application of color, typography, and layout. These images can be understood by business stakeholders, representative users, and engineers alike.

When a prototype is a set of drawings made by a designer at an early stage of the development cycle, it's a tool that is infinitely flexible as well as relatively

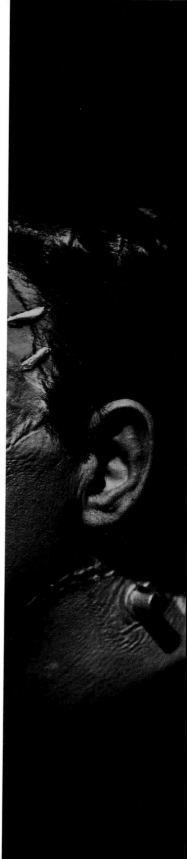

inexpensive. Because no one has a big stake in these drawings, they are not perceived as precious objects, so they encourage debate among members of a project team, and they can be quickly revised.

By drawing a product map, a high-level view of a system, a designer can show how an entire inventory of required features and functions might be organized and displayed. This map can enable technologists, business analysts, product mangers, designers, and even end users to reach a common understanding of exactly what is being built, how the displays will be grouped, how the features will relate to one another, and how the system will be navigated by the people who use it every day. A product map also shows whether the system's organization reflects the business priorities, and whether its content is expressed in a way that is well suited to its context, the workplace where it will be used.

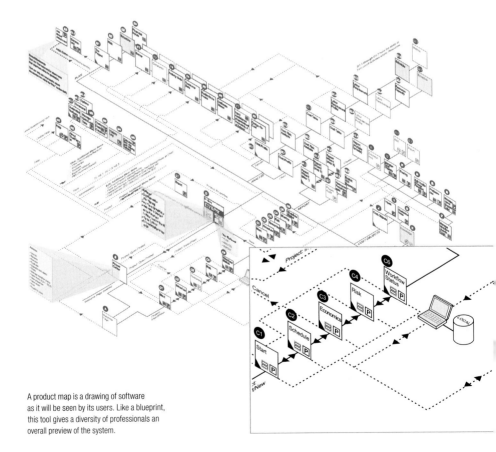

A product map is a drawing of software as it will be seen by its users. Like a blueprint, this tool gives a diversity of professionals an overall preview of the system.

In an agile development process, as the product is developed in increments, product maps allow developers and business stakeholders to
understand how each successive segment will relate to the greater
context of the product. The product map is also an affordable means
of planning longer-term strategies of application design, because it
permits teams to describe how the initial version of the product can
be modified to incorporate future updates and enhancements.

Collaboration and iteration will evolve a product map to a refined
and unified view of the system's overall user interface design.
Ultimately it will inventory the system's displays for subsequent
detailed design. Its structure will dictate what navigational capabilities are required at any position within the system and what broad
set of features, functions, and information each display requires.

Wireframes—detailed drawings of the system's displays—describe
page by page how a product's breadth and depth of features will
come together at the display level. As low-fidelity prototypes, wireframes are a quick, cost-effective way to document functional
requirements while developing a model that can be tested incrementally from multiple perspectives. These drawings, which lack
any suggestion of aesthetic treatment, allow product design and
development teams to focus on issues that are typically left to the
whims of developers and are at the root of user adoption challenges. Issues of language, information versus data presentation,
information hierarchies, management of user context within the
application, and display behaviors all can be resolved by the iterative design of display wireframes.

For business, wireframes can serve many functions. Their rapid
creation and evolution permit early user testing—simple walk-
throughs of tasks. They make it possible to explore alternatives to
data display that may yield important benefits to end users, and in
some projects wireframes can allow for the exploration of multiple
application designs in order to find the optimal direction.

For developers, wireframes provide a reprieve from the painful
experience of trying to imagine what the business wants from the
software based on its written description, and instead enable them
to rally with the business stakeholders around a clear and precise
model of exactly what is described. Wireframes also give the developers an early opportunity to validate business and user desires

against the realities of the technical requirements. In a truly enlight-ened development process, these designs will influence the definition of back-end and middle-system information architectures.

Wireframes are not new, but when they are drawn and managed by design professionals, they become something far more useful than illustrations to accompany the prose of traditional requirements documents or the pictorial counterparts of what developers and business analysts think a system should be and how users should interact with it. Wireframes are tools. They are only as valuable as the skills of those who use them.

Images that show how color will be used are called aesthetic models. A series of iteratively evolving product maps, then wireframes, then aesthetic models keeps the diverse members of a design and development team focused on design decisions in a meaning-ful and appropriate sequence. This means that there will be no subjective debate over whether the color green is an appropriate choice until the team has agreed on the business of the displays themselves. Once consensus is reached, aesthetic models provide an opportunity to develop a detailed specification to support the coding of the displays.

Because these visual prototypes are nothing more than sketches, they can easily be refined. Through a process of iteration, high-level structural diagrams can drive the refinement of a user's work space within a system, while wireframes articulate the details on the screen in a manner that is clear to everyone.

As the visual displays of a system take form, another important characteristic of the design process can occur: innovation. Because a designer's prototype is so pliable and iteration so affordable, there is time to ask, *Is there a better way to do this?* Multiple ideas can be sketched and evaluated simultaneously, and their benefits can be weighed against the cost of implementation.

This process of prototyping and defining the physical displays—sketching out and analyzing the possibilities—leads to consensus, a shared vision of the system that is endorsed by business stake-holders and technologists alike. These cycles of collaborative review and refinement also make it possible to find ways to transform the presentation of data into actionable information and to create a blueprint for a business tool that will be quickly put to use.

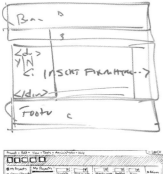

A designer's sketch translates business and user needs into a display framework.

Refined sketches begin to detail the functional requirements.

Black-and-white wireframes are used as testing models to confirm that the system will deliver what's needed in a way that's expected.

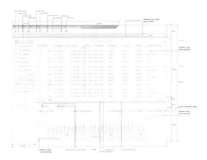

An aesthetic model shows how the data can be clarified by adding color and refining the design.

Detailed visual specifications leave nothing to chance.

Rethinking and Redrawing

One of an artist's greatest challenges is to draw the human figure. The body's soft curves of flesh and muscle with its underlying rigid structure of bones, its variation from individual to individual, its capacity for a range of positions, and its potential for transformation by a simple change of light create challenges that perhaps can never be fully mastered by any artist.

Despite the complexity of the human form, and perhaps because of our familiarity with it, most viewers can easily spot with their untrained eyes a detail in a figure drawing that doesn't seem true. It's not uncommon for an artist who strives to create an accurate, lifelike drawing of the human form to draw and redraw a line over and over to represent the bend of a wrist or the turn of a neck. Line after line is drawn, one on top of the other, until the right line is found: drawn perhaps more heavily than would be ideal, or somewhat less exactly than planned, but visible, there—the line that the artist was looking for, to be considered, studied in relationship to other lines, and understood for the next attempt at mastery of the human form.

What is happening in the mind of the artist who is working to find that line is a rapid cycle of *observation* (analyzing the subject), *action* (moving pencil or charcoal over paper), *evaluation* (comparing the mark just drawn with the observed subject and with the other lines in the drawing), and, if the line is a success, *planning* for the next line to be drawn. The artist moves through this sequence quickly, stopping at any moment to repeat a step until a form emerges from the page through the orchestration of hundreds of lines and thousands of decisions.

The artist's agility in committing a mark to paper—evaluating that mark for its ability to represent a three-dimensional form on a flat sheet of paper, then deciding to redraw that mark or move on to other details, revisiting the mark if necessary and reworking it if needed—is precisely the flexibility needed to explore the possibilities of any design challenge. Graphic design, industrial design, and architecture all share drawing and its characteristics of exploration at the core of their process. The immediacy, the freedom to take risks, the opportunities to change course, and the clarity of expression that drawing provides are exactly what is missing from the way in which most software tools are imagined, formed, and implemented.

SURVEY THE LANDSCAPE

The key to developing more efficient business tools is to understand what the people who will use these tools are currently doing—how they are performing their tasks and why they are working in these ways. An accurate understanding of existing work processes, the people, their environment, and their tools can reveal a tremendous amount of information about what the future must be.

Capturing a true picture of the current state is tricky and has traditionally been a stumbling point for system developers, because the means of attaining this information is often beyond the capabilities of the individuals assigned to perform the assessment. In most system design and development efforts, requirements for new work methods, features, and functions are likely to be gathered by relying on the assumptions of industry experts or by asking workers to endorse those assumptions rather than by objectively observing and evaluating the workforce, their environment, and the current character and quality of their work. Without an analysis to provide an accurate benchmark, the result will be inaccurate and incomplete specifications—marching orders that contain an inventory of wants without an understanding of needs. This can cripple the workers' ability to use a tool and can make it impossible for a system to fulfill its promise.

If you ask people to describe the work they do, you're not likely to hear an accurate description. Instead, you'll probably hear workers describe some idealized, more efficient version of their job and their actual performance—an inventory of tasks executed quickly and efficiently, without delays or mistakes. Even if you're lucky enough to hear an exact description of work processes, you're not likely to be given details that can bring important issues to light.

A data-entry clerk who uses a certain software application may very clearly and confidently describe her work as a tidy sequence of tasks. What she may not mention are the 23 Post-it notes stuck to her monitor to remind her of her password, phone numbers for various company support centers, and system commands to access screens of data and functionality. She may not think to tell you that she uses a handheld calculator to figure out percentages when she receives certain types of customer inquiries. She may not tell you how often she's interrupted in the course of her day. She probably will omit many other details that she assumes are unimportant, and she may withhold information that she doesn't want you to know.

For these reasons, it's important for trained observers to visit the workplace, record their findings, and use this data to model the current state of the work landscape. This model can be used to identify and preserve the most positive characteristics of the current state while weeding out inefficiencies and removing roadblocks to a better future. It can also serve any effort to compare the dissonance between existing methods and those proposed by a business system product.

Designers, psychologists, and anthropologists are trained observers whose research skills extend beyond those of an average visitor to a workplace. These professionals are trained to accurately observe and record the details of human behavior while simultaneously asking why. These observers will focus on discrete areas that business analysts and their consultants typically overlook but which are critical to the definition of what a system must do in order to succeed.

Work processes are only as tidy and as predictable as the humans who do the work.

One area that's commonly overlooked is language. The nouns and verbs that are native to a workplace are incredibly powerful tools that can make the difference between a successful system and one that will require workers to be taught an entirely new language, a language that business analysts and software developers have arbitrarily or ineffectively presented on the screen.

When employees looking for information about the company's vacation policy must learn to search their corporate intranet for "Holidays," this seemingly trivial disparity carries real penalties in lost productivity. Knowing that target audiences associate family leave information with sick days may not be an obvious association for system developers, but could save time and money after deployment. Trained observers who understand the goals and the limitations inherent in large enterprise systems can easily identify gaps between the choice of words and displays that seem logical to system developers and those that seem intuitive to users.

A genuine understanding of important human and cultural characteristics is absolutely critical to successfully deploy any tool into the workplace. But all too often, the attempt to reach that understanding is focused on the rather abstract structures of business processes instead of the more complete human context.

Sometimes an impediment to the success of a system can be removed just by doing some research to find out what people are really thinking and how that might be driving what they are doing. When executives of a large international bank were having trouble getting their sales staff to adopt a new tool for customer-relationship management (CRM), they suspected that the system had a design flaw. The bank had invested a great deal of research in selecting the system from a crowded field of candidates and had spent more than $200,000 to license and deploy it. Unfortunately, most members of the sales force simply weren't using it. My company was asked to evaluate the tool and to fix what the bank managers believed to be problems with usability.

When one of our design researchers first examined the design and the usability of the CRM system independent of the users, he found the system to be a pretty well-designed tool. Its presentation of data, functionality, and ease of navigation were all well considered, and it was far easier to use than most systems of its type. But why then weren't the bank's sales representatives using it?

The next stop in the investigation was to talk with members of the bank's sales staff, the community of end users. Here we found the answer. Almost unanimously, members of the sales force agreed that the CRM tool was easy to use. Unfortunately, it soon became evident that they were struggling with the very idea of the tool. These sales professionals feared that they might lose their jobs if they were not recognized as valuable to the company, and they viewed it as risky to hand over their customer and prospect information to the bank.

The sales representatives were wondering what might happen if they entered the contents of their notebooks, planners, and diaries into the new CRM system—confidential information about their clients' businesses, stock portfolios, marital property, and trust funds, as well as carefully compiled personal details such as clients' birthdays, anniversaries, the names of their children, the names of their favorite golf courses and sports teams, and their favorite brands of scotch. With this information on file, might the bank have less need for some of its current sales reps? Might this information be handed off to other sales reps as the bank thinned staff to improve its numbers?

The well-designed tool was languishing not because of a poor design but because of a failure to fully consider its human audience. A trip into the field early on would have provided valuable insights that could have guided education and training programs to mitigate fears and show the sales force that this new tool offered them opportunities to improve their individual performance, increase their personal value to the bank, and attain greater job security.

The standard process of requirements gathering in software development doesn't encourage discoveries about the context in which a system is deployed, because the process doesn't routinely include professionals with the skills and the techniques to explore the human requirements. Objective observers can recognize unstated business needs by analyzing the ways in which people do their work and by identifying assumptions that conflict with reality. Without this opportunity for discovery, a system's definition will be limited to the known, a space whose parameters are defined by business experts and technologists alone—a landscape whose constricted boundaries stop short of innovation.

PICTURE IT!

When a team of business and technology experts have accurate information about both the business requirements and the human requirements, they have a sound basis for further analysis, collaboration, and innovation. But the way in which this information is represented to them is as important as the accuracy of the data itself.

To obtain software that will fully support the work that needs to be done, it's essential not only to understand that work but also to find ways to accurately describe it. Many techniques are used to depict business processes, including workflow diagrams, use cases, and swim lane diagrams. These diagrams can show the pattern and sequence of actions, decisions, and outputs that must be made in a manufacturing process from concept to fulfillment, and they can illustrate the relationships between the functions of every department throughout a large multinational. But these simplified, highly abstracted representations of work processes are incomplete, because they fail to adequately describe a key element—the people who do the work. Although these drawings may be clear portraits of business processes, they leave a host of important issues unresolved.

Business process diagrams don't capture a snapshot of the interactions among individuals and groups of individuals, their physical environment, the potential impact of a new system on their existing work processes, their experiences with previous deployments of new technology, or their receptiveness to the challenges a new system will pose. Yet it is the individuals who use a system who are directly responsible for its success. The performance of a system will depend on their willingness to adapt to change and to adopt a new system, no matter how forcefully they are encouraged to do so. The sales representatives who refused to adopt their bank's new CRM system had endured an increasingly heavy set of penalties levied for their stubbornness, and at one point their expense reimbursements had even been withheld until their use logs showed a high frequency of record creation and maintenance. They had begun to wonder if perhaps thumbscrews were next.

Illustrations of business processes look very different when they are informed by an understanding of the workforce and pictured as interactions among people. Designers can quickly construct accurate drawings of current work processes that clearly show logjams, redundancies, and conflicts. When those work processes are witnessed and analyzed by design researchers and other trained observers who can objectively evaluate the group of individuals who do the work—their technical know-how, their access to existing information and equipment, and their style of interpersonal communication—these insights can be incorporated into a collaborative process of design that can solve problems at the prototype stage.

What if you could see a model of work processes that allowed you to evaluate the effectiveness of interpersonal communication in a current work process? What if an analysis of work processes enabled you to identify problems that could easily be solved by reconfiguring an existing application and by improving the performance of some other equipment in the workplace? Could such a model also display the time span in which certain tasks are completed and diagram the physical spaces where the work is performed?

The prototyping capabilities of designers are not limited to creating physical artifacts. Their analysis of complex environments can give a multidisciplinary team of professionals a more complete picture of the current business landscape and a better understanding of why things happen as they do. Business analysts possess deep expertise in specific domains, and when they partner with professionals who are trained to observe business processes and ask questions about what they see, they can gain access to a comprehensive set of components for designing a clear map to a better future.

It's not the designer's role to replace a professional who has expertise in a specific area of business or to dictate a solution. Designers apply their skills of observation and use their strengths as analysts and illustrators to supply a broad team of professionals with prototypes that the entire team can use to gain a common understanding of concepts and thoroughly explore alternatives. A designer's prototypes—whether low-fidelity drawings of product maps on a whiteboard, never-before-seen diagrams of observed work patterns, or high-fidelity models of display sequences rendered in full color—are affordable, effective artifacts that can uncover unstated needs, drive out inaccurate assumptions, and encourage genuine innovation.

Showing Why

It's said that decision support is one of the greatest benefits that business systems bring to an organization. Our technological capacity to accumulate and analyze data enables us to frame business decisions in the context of current trends and to construct predictive models of what might happen next. But the data can show much more than what is happening; it also can show *why*.

Consider the data of a hospital's patient transfer report. This is a spreadsheet of facts—dates, times, locations, and numbers that identify patients and record their transfers within a hospital. The value of this data asset is immense if it is used to answer specific questions, such as: *How many patients moved directly from the ICU to the rehabilitation unit in the past 30 days? When did patient X transfer to the ICU?* However, if you do not have a specific question in mind, this data array does little more than serve as an inventory of patient movements, one line of data after another. What can this data tell you without your having to ask?

When a designer makes an inventory of all the hospital's locations and draws lines representing the frequency of transfers between those locations, it immediately becomes apparent that the flow of traffic is concentrated between certain pairs of locations, and the majority of movement seems to involve a dozen or so locations. When seen this way, the data suggests further questions: *What are these locations of high patient movement? Are these locations physically near one another? How does all this traffic relate to rates of infection and mortality? What is the timing of this movement, and what are the cost implications?*

Business needs more than data. Designers can interpret and translate the data into visual forms that reveal patterns, and these patterns can provide better support for decisions—decisions about how to reorganize workflows to make routine tasks easier, more effective, and perhaps safer.

EIGHT

REFRESH THE SYSTEM

Last year, as the greatest economic downturn since the Great Depression dramatically unfolded, numerous CIOs called me to discuss a critical aspect of their jobs that had changed overnight.

Their charter had always been to increase the effectiveness of the professionals within their respective companies, but now they had to do this with little or no budget. Gone were thoughts of purchasing new systems or developing bespoke tools for individual departments. Talk was no longer of software solutions, but of survival. A lot of money had been spent on technology during the good times, and now the return from that investment must be realized—every cent. The conversation was now about how to optimize assets that they currently owned.

Existing business tools very often represent a great deal of potential. The trick is to develop this potential.

It's possible to completely transform some business systems for their constituencies of end users simply by retooling the user interface. Homegrown systems can become vastly more effective by redesigning the software's displays, and large-scale enterprise systems may benefit from an analysis and reconfiguration of on-screen language. If the technology platform for an existing system is solid, what's needed for a better business system may be only skin deep.

The bigger your system, the more flexibility you may have, but even a single application that is sold by subscription may offer opportunities for configuration that can dramatically help performance—improvements that can be made without buying an upgrade or investing in customization.

Think about delaying any new purchase or system development until you can undertake a design review to discover exactly why an existing system is underperforming. There's a good chance that you can squeeze significantly more benefit from an existing system if the design of the user interface is evaluated and improved. If the challenge is user adoption and user effectiveness, the solution may cost only a few thousand dollars and a few weeks of effort. It's likely that the benefits will greatly exceed the cost of a new system. For suggestions on how to identify design talent in-house and lead a design review, see Appendix A, on page 215, "Maximizing Your Design Resources."

If your system is running but you're not satisfied with the results, this chapter provides some low-tech ways to locate the source of the problems and remove impediments that are slowing everyone down.

Only when you've learned to locate and identify the wrench in the system can you eliminate it, or at the very least relocate it to a place where it won't cause active discomfort.

FIND OUT HOW THEY REALLY FEEL

You trained them to use this tool, and now your staff members are working with it every day. Did the training stick? Are people finding the value in this tool? Do they even understand why you deployed it?

If you don't know how your people really feel about the system (and you may not, because whatever you've heard may represent just the tip of the iceberg), the first step is to find out. Don't expect your intranet or enterprise system to draw the adulation that the latest Wii title might; after all, this is work. Have reasonable expectations—but have expectations. A tool shouldn't be a constant irritant. Frustration that surfaces around a business system is a symptom of a problem, but you won't be able to find a cure until you understand the reasons for the frustration.

Observe people using the system to do their work. If the tool has been running in your organization longer than six months, ask a few of its users to think aloud as they interact with it. Ask them to describe what they are doing and why. Some active users may be able to clearly explain how the tool suits their needs, how they wish it could be adjusted to correspond to the way they do their work at present, and the ways in which they would like to do their work. You may need to draw information out of others who have become so accustomed to the idiosyncrasies of the tool that they're unaware of how poorly it suits their needs.

For some professionals, the difficulty of using a system can become a fact of life, a chronic condition that is no longer an obvious impediment to their success. Over time, human beings can learn to tolerate a great deal. I have a friend who was once hit by a car, and for the year following the accident, her job performance declined, her interests in hobbies and activities waned, and her personal relationships steadily deteriorated. During a routine checkup her doctor asked her how things were going. As she spoke she realized that since the accident her life had been slowly coming apart. The doctor recognized the situation and suspected that she was still suffering pain from the accident. He immediately referred her to a specialist who was able to diagnose the source of my friend's pain—pain that had been so constant that gradually she had become unaware of it. With treatment, her pain was eliminated and her life improved dramatically.

If you're running a system that was deployed less than six months ago, you won't need to ask your people how they feel about it; just listen. Be warned: These forays into the field are not recommended for anyone who has a delicate constitution. Nurses, doctors, call-center representatives, sales reps, and most other end users can be brutally honest when they vocalize their feelings about cumbersome, counterintuitive, and ultimately counterproductive business systems foisted upon them. Don't be shocked if, as I have seen on many occasions, you find yourself among a user community that is simply not using the tool at all. In this situation, don't retreat—dig in and find out why. Be prepared to listen. Don't take it personally, and don't defend the application or all the well-intentioned decisions that brought the system to its current form. If members of the user community are expressing dissatisfaction with how the tool works or how they are expected to interact with it, it's obvious that the wisdom of all of the decisions to install the system has been lost on these individuals.

Don't take one person's word for it. Talking with and observing five or six or seven individuals will let you see patterns in the types of things that are challenging the entire population of users. Go to the desks of target users who are performing work associated with the areas of concern. Introduce yourself and ask their permission to watch as they work. Don't be afraid to ask questions as you observe, but be careful not to ask leading questions, and don't ask users to diagnose the problem or propose a solution. You are only interested in observing—and perhaps hearing an opinion.

It's possible that you'll discover a smoldering romance between your users and one of your outdated systems. Some communities of users become unreasonably attached to legacy systems that represent older, less efficient technologies and even more inefficient user interfaces. This can happen when workers become workaround wizards who have learned to master the quirks of a system and integrate it into their jobs, however uncomfortably. Efforts to revise or uproot these systems can be met with resistance, and some businesses compromise by allowing an interface to persist or even to lead the definition of a new system, all in the name of doing right by the end users.

CHECK FOR PHYSICAL EVIDENCE

The workplace can provide a great many clues about how effectively business software is being used. Post-it notes can provide clues as telltale as fingerprints at a crime scene.

Users who are unwilling or incapable of retaining an understanding of how to use a counterintuitive system will be quick to devise support mechanisms. Very often these take the form of Post-it notes attached to a monitor, a keyboard, or semipermanently mounted to a desk with tape. In a feeble attempt to help users, some system manufacturers and development teams try to beat them to the punch by delivering nicely laminated cards and other crutches that are intended to ease people into the system but which often become permanent tools in themselves—the 21st-century equivalents of a wrench on the front seat of a Model T.

Handwritten reminders randomly scattered across desks can provide valuable information. Take copies of them back to your office for analysis to see what they can tell you about stumbling points in the software's design. Identify the tasks users are performing when they reference these notes. Are these tasks frequent or infrequent? Are users looking for support during critical moments? Very often a user's cheat sheets can become the basis of a to-do list for the professionals who are charged with improving the design of a user interface.

If you see words and cryptic sets of alphanumeric characters that you suspect may be passwords, of course there's no need to copy them and risk making someone uncomfortable; their presence is enough to suggest that you should consider asking someone in your communications department to revise the instructions for creating passwords. If your system requires your employees to use multiple passwords to log in, check e-mail, and access other applications,

Clutter on a desktop monitor and passwords posted in plain sight may be cries for help in navigating a confusing system.

explore whether this is really necessary. Implementation of a single sign-on capability may have initially appeared to be an expensive option, but consider how your current password system impacts your struggling employees day to day—not to mention the unsafe practice of leaving passwords around on sticky notes. An investment to design and develop a new sign-on capability may be minuscule in comparison to the cost of wasted time and the risk of security breaches.

MAKE SURE THAT "HELP" IS HELPFUL

Ironically, one of the most common trouble spots in a business system is the place where people go to find help.

Does the help function in your system live up to its name? For that matter, do any of the system's messages that are meant to signal status, correct an action, or provide direction to users in the course of their work really provide the promised support?

Find out what the help system is doing for your users. Is it actually helpful? Is it being used? Is it a crutch for finding other features that are hard to locate? Determine if the help function that is built into the software is indeed serving its purpose. If not, find out where the users are seeking and finding the help they need—whether it's a Web-based source, a help desk staffed by a human being, or that "power user" three cubicles down—and measure the difference between that source and the characteristics of the under-used help tool.

Often a help system does little to support the users as they perform a task because the focus of its content is to describe the features and functions of the system. This model of help content can be useful, but only if users know what they need from the system and how to ask for it. Consider augmenting help content with information specific to your business and the goals of the professionals who are using the tool. A help system that simply exists as a repeat presentation of training materials is likely to be far less useful than content that speaks to the work of the individual.

Review the error messages in your system. It's not helpful to alert users to a condition unless that alert also tells how to address the situation and continue with the task at hand. The software development world still doesn't seem to be convinced that this is necessary. Do the error messages and warnings in your system bring users to a standstill, uneasily waiting to see what might happen next? Or do these messages alert viewers to a problem and tell them in plain English what action they need to take to solve it? Revising the language in error messages can significantly improve a system's usability.

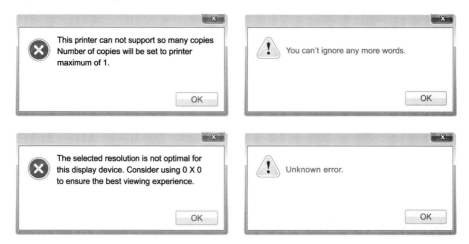

Take a close look at other techniques that may have been employed in an attempt to make the system more user-friendly, and assess their effectiveness. Another leading problem area is the well-intentioned toolbar and its icons. Are the toolbars genuinely helpful, or do they require their unwilling users to undergo an introductory course in cryptography? It's easy to find out. Ask a few users to tell you what each button means, and how often they use it. You may discover that some icons represent valuable functions that would be utilized more often if only the symbols were clearer, while other icons represent little-used functions that should be submerged.

What are the chances that these error messages will be meaningful or useful? It's more likely that they will briefly bring work to a standstill.

Devised as a fast path to often-used features that would otherwise be buried in menu systems, toolbars have recently morphed into complex assemblies of words, buttons and symbols—good intentions with marginal results. Although toolbars are an industry standard, they can be quite problematic. Remember, they're the products of an industry that is still led by engineering. Existing standards for the design of business software should be regarded with great skepticism.

WATCH YOUR LANGUAGE

The language of your business is a concrete and important characteristic to consider when using any software system. Small differences between the terminology on the screen and the words that employees use to communicate with one another across an organization can have significant impact on the effectiveness of the system and the people who use it.

Remember that business software is a communications tool. It sends messages to its users—instructing them how to use the system, why it's relevant to their work, and how their successful operation of the tool will contribute to their success and the success of the organization. It will be the professionals' daily or even minute-by-minute reminder of how something is to be done. It will alert them to certain situations and lead them to appropriate responses. It will tell them where to find things and remind them of their employer's priorities and goals.

A look at the language within a business system can be very revealing. The nouns and verbs that are displayed on the screen may pose unnecessary challenges. Compare the word choices within the displays to the nouns and verbs that are most commonly used in your business and among your workforce—the words used in conversation and interoffice e-mails. Just look, listen, and compare.

Check the names assigned to files within your system. Reports, spreadsheets, and names of documents managed within many enterprise systems are so difficult to remember or even to recognize that the names themselves are barriers to efficient and effective user access. This very obvious issue is often overlooked because of an assumption that "This is just how the system works." This may indeed be the case, but recognize it as an issue and investigate its remedy. Engineers may have defined a naming convention that was

logical to them simply because there was no other recommenda-
tion, and it may be a stumbling block that can be inexpensively
removed. In other cases this may be a difficult issue but one that is
well worth the effort to resolve.

Many business systems provide allowances for configuration of on-
screen language during the installation process. Unfortunately, no
one is usually present in these efforts who is qualified or willing to
add that task to an already complex project. This is why an out-of-
the-box vocabulary is present in so many systems, and it explains
why the words displayed on the user interface of your system may
contain unfamiliar terminology. Check the configuration options
for your system's displays—there may be considerable latitude for
alternatives to system defaults.

RETHINK THE FORM

If your existing system is underperforming, consider the form of
the data on-screen or within the reporting output.

Do sample reports, graphs, and charts communicate information
beyond the data itself? Do they tell you things clearly and directly,
or is the user of the report responsible for decoding the messages
that lie within the data? Improving the presentation of the data may
offer significant opportunities to increase its value.

ELIMINATE CLUTTER

Sometimes all that is needed to make a job move more quickly is a
bit of reorganization.

I once had the opportunity to observe data-entry professionals at
an office where they processed insurance claims. Their job was
to transfer handwritten data from paper forms completed by customers into the company's electronic claims-processing system,
entering the information from each printed form into a series of
data fields on their desktop screens.

The printed form was clearly organized and easy to follow, and it
was obvious that it had been painstakingly designed. This was a
wise business decision, as it no doubt minimized errors by customers who were under stress because of the circumstances of their
claims and who might easily have become frustrated by the task of

completing an unfamiliar form. This well-designed form encouraged accurate, legible completion on the part of the customers, which helped the data-entry clerks to execute their task accurately and rapidly.

Unfortunately, the on-screen displays looked so dramatically different from the printed forms that it was difficult to see how they were meant to serve as a repository for the customers' information.

Even a virtual desktop can get in the way of a user's productivity. An understanding of the user can lead to gains in efficiency.

Data fields were presented in an order that was different from their printed counterparts; the screen prominently displayed fields that were seldom used for the data-entry task; and colored boxes and lines that were intended to group related elements in the displays only served to create distracting visual noise. The more experienced claims processors had learned to use the tab key on their keyboards to skip unnecessary display fields; they had realized that after they completed certain fields, one or two or even three strokes of the tab key would be necessary before they could move past unnecessary fields and begin typing information into the next appropriate field.

The solution was simply to eliminate the clutter by moving rarely used and inappropriate fields out of the way so that the users could navigate field by field through the screen, according to how the data needed to be input. Graphical treatments such as colored boxes and lines were removed, except for those that clarified the display.

CONSIDER THE CONTEXT

Your firsthand observations may reveal unexpected, nontechnical solutions that can boost user performance. As you observe work in progress, look beyond what you see on the screen and consider whether some fixes can be made within some of the work processes that relate to your existing technology.

The claims processors who were faced with awkward displays on their desktops had learned to cope with the disconnect between those displays and the paper forms. But in addition, these professionals were encumbered by piles of printed forms on their laps. Yes, the work queue—a stack of paper forms—was resting on each user's lap throughout the process of data entry. Some users sat sideways at their workstations in order to accommodate the papers; others sat forward, leaning over the pile of forms on their laps to reach the keyboard and entering data by reading the form on top of the stack of paper between their two extended arms. These physical contortions were remedied with a bit of workspace organization. All that was needed was a little initiative to shift around some office equipment to make room to rest the paper forms on desktops, next to monitors and keyboards—letting the workers pull up to their desks and type comfortably.

Knowing more about the user's workplace can reveal ways to modernize archaic work processes beyond the screen.

Find out how the physical workspace is affecting work processes, and consider the ways in which the experience, the knowledge, the language, and the culture of the workforce is influencing their ability to use the tools at hand.

TAKE THE MEASURE OF THE PROBLEM

Quantitative measurements can provide additional insight into how well a system is performing and how it can be adjusted to better serve the business and its users. Electronic server-side measuring tools can precisely monitor usage within an enterprise system. From the back end, these tools can monitor the actions of individuals as well as the movements of whole populations of users—tracking each step they take to perform certain tasks and showing exactly how quickly and how frequently they complete those tasks. A host of other tools are available to analyze Web site traffic by identifying the navigational patterns of visitors to the site. These measurements provide insight into what people are doing, alerting an organization to areas of the system that are heavily used and others that are seldom used, and showing precisely where users are exiting a system before completing a process.

These quantitative tools are less likely to reveal why some areas of a system enjoy tremendous use and others are almost never used. Although it might seem that heavy use is good use, heavy traffic in a certain area could mean that users are making the same mistake again and again—increasing the use metrics but simultaneously reflecting a rising level of user frustration.

There are numerous ways to complement the server-side usage data with a qualitative assessment of *why* certain patterns have emerged. The most obvious method is simply to observe the system in use, keeping in mind what the server logs have revealed about user performance. By complementing these observations with carefully crafted questions and an appreciation for the overall context of the users, a process of diagnosis can begin to balance the quantitative information about what parts of the system need to be fine-tuned with qualitative answers as to *why* professionals are interacting with the system the way they are.

Another way to obtain more detailed explanations is through formalized user testing. Usability experts can plan structured tests that will engage users in specific tasks in a controlled environment. A carefully crafted testing plan will arrange for individuals to use a system while their performance is measured and recorded for further analysis. These tests can be used to answer questions as broad as *How effectively does this system support its users in doing their work?* or as discrete as *How many seconds does it take to execute this task?* Specialized hardware that has been developed for usability testing can record keystrokes and track movements of the human eye as users scan the screen of a desktop monitor, allowing us to see movements so small that the users themselves are not even aware of them.

Remember that looking to technology alone for an understanding of how a system is performing will provide only part of the answer. Be sure to balance these metrics with an understanding of how the tool is working in the hands of your professionals.

DEFINE YOUR PRIORITIES

Make sure to rank the types of problems you learn about according to their impact on the business. A problem associated with a minor task that is performed once a week needs to be weighed carefully against a seemingly trivial hiccup that impacts a routine function that is executed every hour by dozens (or thousands) of individuals.

Do the math: For each design flaw you discover, how many people are affected? How often? What is the potential impact? What are the risks to the integrity of the data? What are the risks to the business?

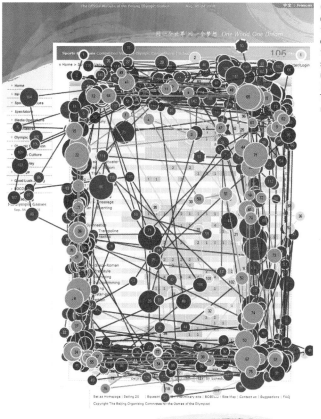

Computer hardware can precisely track the eye movements of multiple users as they scan identical screens, with each user represented by a distinct color. The patterns are noticeably similar.

GET AN OUTSIDE OPINION

Trust your gut, but remember that self-diagnosis can be tricky. If you search the Web to figure out why your back aches, you might become convinced that you need a kidney transplant, but your doctor may be able to tell you that you just need to sit up straighter at your desk.

Ask the contractor who just remodeled your offices to inspect the job for quality and code compliance, and that inspection may not be as thorough or as objective as one performed by an licensed inspector. If the same business analysts and technologists responsible for the design and deployment of your existing system are called upon to identify and remedy its flaws, don't expect a dramatic transformation.

High-level assessments and observations of work processes, language, and screen displays offer good ways to consider whether the system you have could benefit from a more detailed analysis and redesign in order to improve its performance without replacing it. An objective observer may be able to see that a problem in one area originates elsewhere, just as your physician may be able to diagnose the ache in your arm as the result of an injury to your shoulder.

After taking a close look at your existing system, it may be worthwhile to call in a usability specialist or a designer—or both—to arrange a more formal polling of the system's users, to help prioritize problem areas, and to lead a process to refresh and restart the system. For advice on how to evaluate a consulting design company or usability expert, see Appendix B, on page 219, "Tough Questions for Consultants."

NINE

YOUR NEXT SYSTEM

Sooner or later, you'll be thinking about a new system. Whether you buy or build, this is a great opportunity. Products in the marketplace may bring to light methods you haven't considered, and they also may offer more comprehensive data storage and retrieval capabilities than you ever could have imagined for your business.

Once you've narrowed the field of candidates to products represented by reputable manufacturers and confirmed that the systems have solid technical architecture and sound code, it makes sense to evaluate the systems just as you would any other prospective purchase. Business software has a cost of ownership that may bear little relation to its value, and the answers to a few good questions are worth a thousand promises.

In this chapter you'll find the most valuable questions you can ask to obtain the greatest return on your investment.

WHAT IS THIS THING?

If the product is a time-reporting solution, a data warehouse, or any of the multitudes of packaged "solutions" on the market, make sure that every facet reflects an understanding of your business and your professionals, from the executive suite to the loading dock.

Will terminology on-screen and the metadata that will store descriptions and keys to the data repositories resonate across your organization? Will this system help to clarify the complexity of tasks? Is this really a tool, or is it possibly a technological barrier that will prevent members of your team from realizing their full potential?

Just because a system is already installed in other companies in your line of business doesn't necessarily mean that it's *working* in those companies. Make sure you are looking at a proven solution, one proven on every level—technological performance, business efficiency, and acceptance by end users.

If the tool you're considering has been retrofitted from a related business, ask about what changes were made. If it was initially developed for a business different from your own, think carefully about your end users. The transactions that the system supports and the structures of its database may translate to your business, but the display tier may speak another language. I have watched many clients, in seeking innovative new solutions for their companies, look to systems designed and developed for businesses outside their own industries. Most of the time the display tier is the area that is least carefully considered, when in truth it's one of the most sensitive aspects of a potential deployment.

IS THIS WHAT WE REALLY NEED?

The sales pitch is as old as time—salespeople hawking a hundred varieties of snake oil that "you can't do without." But your accounting office or order fulfillment team may not work precisely like any other, and that brand-name manufacturer of enterprise systems may not have the right answer for your business.

If you fully understand your business, its processes, and your employees, your requirements for a business system are clear. With a well-defined set of requirements in hand, the noisy marketplace

A powerful pitch for a simple solution can be persuasive.

of candidate systems is far safer to negotiate, and there is less risk that product manufacturers will use their lists of product capabilities to dictate your definition of needs.

Assess how closely a product and its manufacturer's promises measure up to the future as you see it. Any gap between what you need and what a vendor has to sell must be completely understood in order for you to accurately predict whether your organization and its professionals will benefit from a tool and whether the vendor's promises will be fulfilled. You can make your own yardstick to measure various facets of candidate systems by drafting a prototype of an ideal or best-case solution. By spending a small amount of time up front with a designer, you may be able to prototype the ideal dashboard, account display, or reporting interface, and in doing so, set a bar that any candidate system must clear.

The problem with many systems can be traced all the way back to the beginning, when a company heads into the marketplace with a seriously flawed set of requirements in hand. For decades, businesses have relied upon requirements documents to evaluate new software systems and to develop custom products. Everything about these documents—from the process used to create them to their physical form—will influence the success of the final product, and unless they are properly prepared, you may find that you have staked a large and critical investment in the future of your business on very shaky ground.

A requirements document is commonly based on information from polls of target users, conjecture on the part of various business experts and user proxies, and exhaustive mapping of the business operations by business analysts. At best, a requirements document may be a request to subtly improve the status quo for the end user by installing some latest and greatest back-end technology. At its worst it may be a wholly inaccurate description of an essential system that should be bought or built. Very likely it won't describe the level of innovation the business needs or the innovation that this opportunity affords.

To be sure that you have an accurate description of what you need, make sure that professionals with the right skills have applied appropriate investigative techniques. Ask the wrong question, and the answer is irrelevant. Trained observers such as designers and design researchers can help business experts look beyond what has been accepted within the organization as common knowledge—assumptions and beliefs that may be misleading—to develop a set of requirements that are grounded in a true understanding of the business, its people, and their combined potential.

A $100 Million Guinea Pig?

To say that America's largest waste hauler was disappointed with its investment in a new enterprise system would be a $100 million understatement.

Early in 2005, Waste Management Inc. began exploring ways to acquire a system that would streamline its operations and improve revenues—ideally, an out-of-the-box system that wouldn't require customization. After seeing several demonstrations from SAP, which had previously licensed waste-management software in some European countries, the company signed a licensing agreement with SAP, which provided that the software would be implemented by the end of 2007.

In March 2008, Waste Management Inc. sued SAP AG and SAP America for fraud, charging that its system was unsuited to the U.S. market and that the product was a "complete failure," unable to run even the company's most basic revenue-management operation.

Waste Management charged that SAP had presented "fake, mock-up simulations" to win the contract and that the U.S. version of the software was "undeveloped, untested, and defective."

Alleging that it had been used as a guinea pig by SAP to gain entry into the U.S. waste market, Waste Management sought to recover more than $100 million in costs as well as damages.

In hindsight, it's reasonable to ask:

Was it realistic to expect that an out-of-the box solution would fit the company's specific needs?

Were SAP's references checked? How much information did SAP provide about its American and European customers within the waste management industry?

What differences between the U.S. and European markets could significantly affect the performance of an enterprise system developed specifically for one industry?

What provisions did the licensing agreement contain to guarantee functionality and other promises made during SAP's marketing pitch? Did the contract contain an escape clause?

Could end users have sat in front of SAP's foreign market screens and observed what Waste Management's executives couldn't have seen?

The case was pending at the time of this writing.

WILL THE BASIC MODEL DO THE JOB?

Think about a child's first bicycle. In a bicycle shop you'll find no end of accessories—baskets (front and back), brightly colored panniers, bells, spoke covers, lights, and handlebar tassels. The options go on and on. And if you're foolish enough to take your young son or daughter with you to buy that first bike, the combination of a hungry salesperson and an excited child might result in your leaving the store with an accident about to happen. That first bike might look like the best-kitted-out pair of wheels on the street. But that collection of extras may make it difficult to ride the bike, especially for your beginner.

Almost certainly those add-ons will make learning a greater challenge than it might be without them. Once mastered, the next question is, will these baskets, bags, and bells ever be of use to the child? Surely the most sensible approach would be to introduce these features gradually, as the rider masters the fundamental task, strengthens basic skills, and develops an understanding of the available accessories.

New business systems are flooded with the technical accomplishments of the engineers who have created them in the form of features and functions that a team of well-intentioned business analysts have inventoried as being essential to the users' success with the product. How quickly these features and functions can be understood by their users, and in what order, can greatly influence the tool's success in the hands of those individuals and its contribution to the success of the business.

A well-designed system will seem self-evident to some degree even when users are first introduced to it. Having a basic understanding of the main purpose of the tool allows users to be immediately successful in using and exploring it, while adopting more advanced capabilities according to their ever-increasing comfort with the system. Training efforts, if they are required for the launch of a new system, should not be an exercise in teaching professionals where to find things in the system and how to make sense of a clutter of features and functions. Training should be an opportunity to demonstrate the value of the system to its users.

WHO WILL BE USING IT?

If the professionals who buy or build a system don't possess a clear understanding of the people who will use it, take time to make sure they gain that understanding.

Don't confuse the end users of a system with their managers or professional proxies in the form of so-called experts and analysts. The perceptions and assumptions of these surrogates are highly suspect. A manager's view of a process or a work environment may not take in all the nuances that influence a user's ability to do a job. Business analysts or resident authorities may have outdated views of the target environment and its people, and they may have such strong opinions and firm beliefs in their knowledge of the domain that they are incapable of making discoveries or seeing alternatives to what they believe to be true.

The design and development process of most software relies heavily on abstract models of workflow—tidy, oversimplified drawings depicting neatly boxed tasks linked by precisely drawn arrows. But unless these models represent the people who are responsible for doing the work, workflow modeling is woefully inadequate. To ignore the people who do the work is to design in a vacuum and almost assuredly to err.

Business analysts, in their efforts to define the clearest picture of work, distill an elemental understanding of the business that might compare to describing the human body in terms of 75 percent of its content—water. Without considering the human element, we may have an accurate accounting of 75 percent of what the business is doing, but to ignore the remainder of the content would be to miss its essence.

For a decade or more, software development teams have attempted to describe the human element by using personas to define the archetypal end user of a system. These hypothetical sketches include fictitious information such as name, age, hair color, educational background, marital status, life goals, and even favorite color. Personas can be a reasonable approach to help all the members of a project team to develop a common and general understanding of a diverse group of potential customers within a vast population of target users, such as retail banking customers who will use an

ATM machine, or college students who are prospective users of an online student loan service center. Personas are less useful when an understanding of personal details about a target user isn't balanced by a clear understanding of that user's role within a business organization. In these situations, personas developed to address high-level and somewhat superficial characteristics can have marginal value to a project.

Two separate definitions of a persona are needed within the workplace: the archetypal individual, and that person's *role*—the responsibilities, attributes, and expectations of that person's position within the business. High-level personas may attempt to reach into the psyche of a prototypical human to provide a grounding force for the generation of ideas, an excellent technique for ideation exercises by marketing and advertising. However, business systems require a deep understanding of the individual's professional role, responsibilities, and goals, and the relationship of that role to the performance of others and to the company as a whole.

Although high-level personas can be fun for a team to develop and marginally useful as a periodic checkpoint for decisions that may impact end users, a user profile may be more effective, though less entertaining to develop. Profiles are developed from skilled observation of human beings in context; they are not based on conjecture, fancy, or intuition (the project stakeholders won't be exploring the life goals of the fictitious character or deciding on the hair color of the persona's firstborn). User profiles focus on the relationships among the business, the system, and the target user. A profile will consider the abilities and attitudes of the individual, but it also will detail the characteristics of that individual's corresponding role within the organization.

Profiles document the receptiveness of users to training, the context of their workplace, their positions within a larger business function or work process, and other factors that may affect their ability to successfully operate the system. Profile development also seeks a clear understanding of the title an individual has within the organization and the responsibilities and influences of that title.

Profiles challenge the conventional belief that an industry expert, a retired professional from the trade, or just someone who has

been around the business for a long time can know enough about a job and its human performers to fully represent the users in the process of purchasing or developing software. By extending our understanding of individuals to include consideration of the relationships among roles in a work setting, how reward and success are related to roles, and how these roles are supported by existing tools and methods, profiling provides a more complete understanding of these individuals as they relate to the system, their jobs, and the organization.

Within the health care industry, physicians and nurses often serve as proxies in the design of software systems developed for their counterparts in private hospitals, public clinics, and teaching hospitals. Knowledgeable of their domains, these experts are fluent in the details of their professions. They can explain such things as the significance of systolic and diastolic blood pressure measurements and their normal levels, the importance of closely monitoring any patient being given Digoxin for a heart condition, and the policy that no action in the care of a patient be taken without a direct order from the appropriate professional. These data and work techniques of patient care may be universal and timeless. However, an ever-changing work environment exists wherever communities of human beings are engaged in the performance of a task that is driven by an ongoing need for improved accuracy, effectiveness, and savings. The need to closely monitor the levels of Digoxin in the blood of a patient receiving the drug may be as urgent today as it was 20 years ago, but how a health care professional monitors the data and what actions certain values may trigger must be understood in light of a dynamically changing work environment, updated science, new training methods for health care professionals, an evolving legal landscape, and a host of other influences. These questions extend well beyond the fluency of a single professional in any given field.

It's essential to maintain a constant appreciation for the true representatives of target user audiences throughout the purchasing process or development cycle. Expert proxies for these communities of professionals may be inadequate at best, and at worst they may be seriously misleading. Whatever picture of the end users, their roles, and their work context is being used as a point of reference along the way, be sure it's an accurate image.

WHAT'S IT LIKE TO USE?

This is where the rubber meets the road. When asked this question, many sales representatives for business systems begin to behave more like magicians or infomercial hosts for Ginsu knives than reputable professionals genuinely interested in showing how their products will be useful to your business and its people.

Typically, demonstration systems are rolled out in lecture halls and boardrooms where product representatives take control of the mouse and walk their audiences through an unimaginably easy and wildly productive scenario of system use. The speed and grace demonstrated during these product walk-throughs can be downright intimidating. This is where the emperor's new clothes are presented, fitted, and sold to CIOs, executives, and target users who fail to muster the courage to admit that what they are witnessing doesn't make sense to them.

Caught in a position where promises of "optimized business processes" and more efficient "transaction flows" seem to conflict with their own uneasy sense that *I don't quite get this*, decision makers and target user communities alike sit silently, chalking up that lump of skepticism in their guts to the perpetual disconnect that exists between all technology and mere mortals like themselves. Any inadequacies they sense must be of their own making, not those of the system they see dancing across the demonstration screen.

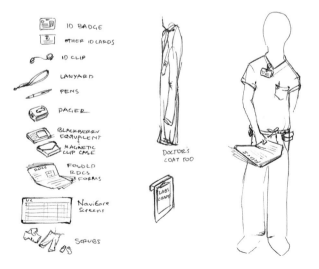

In introducing new technology, it helps to consider what kinds of equipment are currently used. A researcher's sketch shows some of the tools a physician juggles as well as the work clothes where those tools are carried.

Ask a few real users to test the system in the place where they work. Introduce them to the tool and describe its purpose. Then talk them through the execution of a typical task—with their hands on the mouse and keyboard. Make note of their observations. What is making sense to them? What are the challenges? Are the users tripped up by design glitches in the user interface such as unfamiliar terms on the screen, confusing navigation, data displays that are incomplete or too complex? Ultimately, do these professionals seem excited by the prospect of using this tool to succeed in their work, or do they look concerned, or even panicked?

Even if the vendor can't provide a true test-drive, technology can allow simulations of use, particularly if the product's manufacturer is boasting any depth of experience in your vertical market.

If a system vendor tells you that her company invests heavily in the user interface design, make sure it is reflected in the product. Most large software companies employ human factors and design professionals. Some employ hundreds of them. But the influence of these individuals on the product and the way it is designed and developed is minimal. Instead, they work in remediation—fixing problems that result from a faulty product development process led by engineering.

When faced with an inconvenient barrier, many people will find a shortcut even if the alternate path causes wear and tear.

If what you and the end users experience during a test doesn't feel right, it's time for a heart-to-heart talk with your sales representative. If he or she concedes that some of the displays are awkward or the user interface is problematic *some of the time*, ask about remedies for the situation. If the proposed solution is a budget for training or change management, think carefully about the amount of time and money you're prepared to risk to realize the product's promised value. Training programs can be effective, but remember that human beings are unpredictable, and when faced with a system that inhibits their progress, they're likely to seek an alternative path.

ARE THE INFORMATION DISPLAYS INFORMATIVE?

What can the data tell you?

Reporting capabilities—the retrieval and presentation of data sets from vast database stores—are a top business priority, and software companies aggressively promote these capabilities. Decades ago, in the early years of computing, the quick retrieval and presentation of data was indeed a miraculous event, but business systems presented these data in astonishingly raw form, as rows and columns of alphanumeric characters up, down, and across printed pages and within thousands of cells on computer screens that only reluctantly revealed the trends of their business. Unfortunately, not a lot has changed since those early days.

The speed at which business moves in the twenty-first century requires rapid assessment of data and fast action based on that assessment. But even the best data may be slow to tell us what we need to know. Sometimes the trends aren't obvious, and other times we realize that we've been looking in the weeds for things that are in plain sight. When data are presented in a form that can be quickly analyzed, we can dissect the details and find trends, anomalies, and other information that can suggest the best course of action.

If you're evaluating a new system, and if the manufacturer claims to know your business, make sure the vendor knows the difference between serving up data to your professionals and giving them actionable information.

This simple trait—a system's capability to present data in the most appropriate and informative form for its intended audience—can mean the difference between a system that may negatively impact an already suboptimal environment and a system that can significantly enhance your business.

HOW CLEARLY DOES IT COMMUNICATE?

Poor communication by software systems is so ubiquitous that many buyers feel compelled to accept a very low standard despite their reservations:

This system runs "queries," but our people run "reports." I guess they could get used to that. The employees will have to log in to this system with a password that's different from the other system they use. They could learn that, too.

You may be setting yourself up to divert hours from the workday and waste valuable training budgets to teach your target users a new language or to accelerate their understanding of counterintuitive features. If your employees find that their corporate intranet doesn't speak their language, they'll look elsewhere for the information they need, and the system will be unable to deliver on its potential business improvements.

HOW FORGIVING IS IT?

What's it like to make a mistake when you use this system? After all, one thing is guaranteed—human users will make mistakes.

Automobile manufacturers have been building safety and passenger-protection features into their products for decades. They know that accidents happen. They also know that people are concerned with what might happen in an accident, so manufacturers recognize the value of developing equipment and features that speak to

these concerns. Side-curtain airbags and sensors that predict when an accident is about to occur and initiate lifesaving actions before the driver may even be aware of a problem are leading messages in marketing and sales campaigns. For security-minded consumers, these features are compelling reasons to buy certain models.

When a software system rolls out within an organization, many of the instructional messages of training sessions will be forgotten. Assume that some of these forgotten instructions on how to navigate the system will be unimportant; perhaps they even included explanations of some never-used features. But also anticipate the biggies: How do you sign in to the system? What happens if you update the wrong file? What if you mistakenly delete or move a file? How accommodating is the system in such cases?

Demonstration scenarios typically picture a carefree world of error-free use, but ask the sales professionals who showcase the application in product demonstrations and walk-throughs to replicate a typical user error and show how a user would recover from such an event.

HOW WILL IT SUPPORT OUR BRAND?

Will they love us or hate us?

When the system is a publicly facing Web site that enables customers to request information or make a purchase, it's obvious that it is important to give these visitors the best possible experience. Their success or failure and their pleasure or displeasure with the site will be the impression that is recorded with each individual. A heightened sensitivity to this aspect of their brands has pushed Web site owners to monitor and refine both the art and the science of the online experience. A host of technological techniques for performing quantitative assessments of usage patterns and user behaviors, combined with qualitative assessments from surveys and focus groups, can keep site owners aware of every aspect of the customer's interaction with the public face of their corporate identities.

Less obvious for many information technology professionals and the organizations that employ them is the importance of how their colleagues and employees experience internal systems, and the potential impact of those experiences on their brand.

The tools we put into the hands of our employees represent our support of those individuals' success. The desk, the chair, the computer, the software, the building, the company's products, and its advertisements in the marketplace—even the food in the cafeteria—all contribute to an employee's impression of the company. For organizations that settle for delivering suboptimal software for internal use, the damage to the corporate brand is great. How wise are leaders who present their employees with tools that hobble their performance?

It's a great day for me when we roll out new equipment to the employees at my company or cut the ribbon on a newly renovated facility. Better equipment signifies a company's investment in itself, faith in its employees, and its confidence in the future.

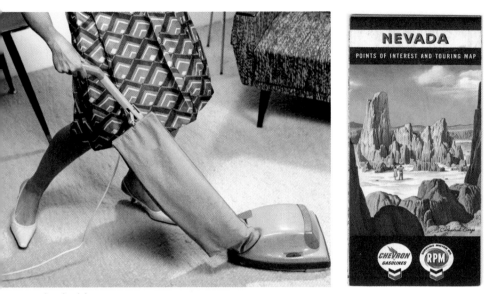

In work and play, products change the way we interact with them as they evolve into new forms.

When investment in infrastructure positively affects the individuals at their desks, the company receives a boost. When the impact is negative, the damage affects the entire company.

IS THIS PRODUCT TRULY INNOVATIVE?

What's happening inside the black box of a system may be innovative. New structures for data storage, faster or more elegant transaction code, and hardware processors that challenge tradition while delivering greater speed are all important types of system innovation. But these are not the sole sources, and they may have only marginal value unless they also enhance a greater system, one that supports the men and women who perform the everyday tasks of the business.

Innovation should be considered in terms of two distinct qualities, behavior and form. Together, these tightly linked and interdependent characteristics offer a good way to sort out the questions required to evaluate a tool.

First, find out what kind of action the system will stimulate. Does this tool transform the very work it supports? Will it encourage or support behaviors that change work processes for the better? Making it possible for workers to fill out a form on a computer screen, field for field, instead of completing it by hand is a small

step forward. In the early days, when business tasks were being computerized, the accuracy and reliability of electronic data capture was viewed as a significant advancement over a paper-based workplace. But a device that changes how people think of a task and how they perform it is truly innovative.

A robotic vacuum cleaner that propels itself around the floor and whose human owner only has to set a timer and periodically empty a dust receptacle is a game changer. The task is radically transformed from one that requires someone to push and pull a machine throughout the performance of the task to a process in which a human must intervene only at the beginning and end.

An in-car navigation system that displays a road map to the driver is an innovation that is only an incremental step away from the cumbersome, awkwardly folded paper maps that we once bought in gas stations. Far more innovative is the behaviorally transformative voice that understands our destination and talks us through the decision points of the optimal route without asking us to take our eyes off the road or our hands off the wheel. Those early GPS maps were a good first step, but their colorful displays of road systems were essentially a computerization of our old ways of referencing the options for traveling from point A to point B, and they continued to distract us from the task of driving. Thanks to the intelligent behaviors of today's navigation systems, the task of navigating the road has been transformed and the use of maps while driving is forever changed.

The second quality of innovation is form. Has the shape of things changed for the better? Formal innovations represent changes to the traditional shape of an object that significantly improve that object's ability to serve its human users. The shift from a paper map to a digital display is one example of a formal change. A much better example is the map of the London Underground, the dramatically simplified map designed by Harry Beck. Through the formal transformation of this object, efficiencies were gained and the experience of using this tool was improved—true innovation.

Innovative forms can change the way we work. Cordless phones severed our physical tether to our desks and allowed us to use this technology while simultaneously interacting with our physical environment as never before. With laptop computers, we still type on a relatively unchanged keyboard and drive a pointer across the screen, but now we can do this work almost anywhere.

In each of these examples, innovation was achieved by rethinking what surrounded the human's basic task. That task was transformed by providing easier access to it—an altogether enhanced experience. With the Underground map, riders continued to experience the service of riding in a rail car between two points. However, with a formally transformed map, using the system to explore new routes and new parts of the city became much easier. Similarly, laptop computers have not necessarily improved the way we compose and manage documents in the files of our computers, but for me, being able to type significant parts of this book in dozens of hotel rooms and in a plane 30,000 feet over the Atlantic represented a formal transformation that freed me to work when and where I chose.

If a product is truly innovative, any formal and behavioral changes that it proposes to introduce must be carefully considered in the context of its target audience. Consider whether the changes are appropriate for that audience, and whether the members of that audience have the ability and desire to adopt the changes. Otherwise, persuading them to adopt those innovations will be another challenge.

WHAT DO TRAINING AND
CHANGE MANAGEMENT REALLY MEAN?

A client once told me that he thought that change management budgets are directly proportional in size to how screwed up you can expect your business to be after the launch of a new system—the more money you need, the bigger the headaches that await your organization after going live. I have seen training budgets support laminated cards that remind employees of the lessons from training, posters celebrating a product's launch, and balloons to decorate an office on the system's first day. This kind of fanfare for a system launch reminds me of Queen Gertrude's line in *Hamlet*: "The lady doth protest too much, methinks."

Leading the deployment of a new system is seldom simple. When computers first appeared on desktops, the challenge was considerable. People who had been working within a centuries-old environment of paper-based records, ledgers, and files were being asked to think about their work in a new way. Word processing applications, with their complex vocabulary of commands, forced people who were accustomed to typewriters and their inherent immediacy to create documents in a far more indirect way. To indent a paragraph while using a typewriter was a simple act of moving a lever, but with word processing, this act, and making any other change in a document, could be achieved only through accurate recall of the system's vocabulary of commands. The adoption of word processing tools in the workplace required training. This was early computing—industry and computer science beginning to connect technological capabilities with desired business benefits.

Most members of today's workforce have grown up with computers, and a generation of people have come of age thinking of a document as an electronic

Perceptive skeptics like Hamlet's mother may think that the fanfare to launch a new system doesn't ring true.

file or an on-screen collection of data. They shop online and play games online against opponents on other continents. They program the thermostats in their homes and even their coffeemakers. Yet even now, as we successfully use more and more technology in every other part of our lives, a history of training for electronic business systems has created an expectation that it's acceptable to require end users and their employers to spend a great deal of valuable time and money on training.

When new consumer products are introduced, training is not a necessity. Apple didn't send me to a class in order to help me realize my potential as an iPod owner, and Viking didn't train me to use its latest oven. Somehow I have successfully integrated these devices into my life, and now I wonder how I ever lived without them. Sure, these devices don't mirror the complexity of a hospital's electronic health records. But neither a household oven nor an iPod enjoys the luxury of a very specific, narrowly focused, highly educated audience of users.

Business systems aren't consumer products, but when considering training, it's useful to think of them as such in order to learn what the proposed training is for, and why it may be critical to the product's success within the organization. Training users to navigate cumbersome menu systems, translate opaque terminology, and deal with unpredictable behaviors is not the stuff of which a training course should be built. A product that requires training so that its users can learn to use a counterintuitive tool is a waste of time and money, but teaching people new methods and processes that will increase their efficiency and effectiveness is money well spent.

If funds are committed to training before and after the launch of a new system, investigate the curriculum to find out how much time and effort will be committed to teaching users about the tool compared with how much training will be dedicated to making them better at their jobs. Even though some companies promote the view that simply using their products will make a worker a better employee, these two things do not always directly relate to one another.

Remember that your target users know your business. They may even know more about the details of the business than those who make the purchasing decisions for the system. Their experience and knowledge of the business should give them a high level of comfort with any new system that purports to be designed for them and their industry.

WHAT REAL INFORMATION DOES THE MANUFACTURER HAVE ABOUT USER ADOPTION AND EFFECTIVENESS?

In an ideal world, any business system deployed within an organization would be required to meet certain standards of user performance. Unfortunately, most licensing agreements guarantee only the technical fidelity of the software, not the ultimate success of the product in the hands of its users.

Ask your vendors whether they have data about user adoption and acceptance of their systems. Can they provide metrics? Can they arrange for you to speak with one of their clients who has installed the system? Better yet, can you speak with a few people who actually use it on a daily basis?

Explore the possibility of defining human performance criteria within your next software contract. This might include specifying employee positions of a certain title or management level, the tasks that those employees will perform, and the time frame in which your company can expect them to be proficient in operating the system. Would it be too much for the supplier of an enterprise system to guarantee that your managers will be able to use it to generate reports—by themselves?

The time required to perform a specific task can be easily measured and averaged across a user population within just a few days. For example, by testing a dozen workers, the time it currently takes to locate certain information within a corporate intranet can be quantified. If the intranet you are considering deploying will be doing little more than serving up thousands of pages of information to your employees, might the supplier of that system be willing to guarantee that the average time for your 50,000 employees to find information about your company's policy on family leave will be no more than 90 seconds?

Even if vendors won't provide data about usability or offer a guarantee that includes user adoption figures, the way they respond to questions about these issues can tell you a great deal.

WHAT ABOUT THOSE SERVICE CONTRACTS AND FUTURE UPGRADES?

To avoid disruption to their business, many organizations forgo incremental upgrades and releases that they are entitled to receive as part of their licenses. Very often the initial installation was such a trying experience that no one is willing to plunge into tinkering with whatever "success" has been achieved. Instead, businesses pay their annual upgrade fees as contracted, and move ahead without actually deploying the upgrades. The risks are just too high and the value to the business is just not clear enough to warrant venturing out on that path.

Can the system vendor provide a picture of that annual decision point? Technical upgrades and descriptions of enhanced product features are normally touted at these times. Ask if the product vendor uses design processes that will allow you to see a complete picture of what the annual upgrade will provide. Can you anticipate how upgrades will impact the end user community—from a high-level perspective as well as a detailed, screen-level perspective? Will technical upgrades be framed in terms of their real business advances or their benefits to the users, or will they represent only technological innovation?

Today's purchase will have implications well beyond tomorrow. Make sure your vendor can chart and deliver the future of the system in ways that correspond with the future of your business— from the perspectives of technological sophistication, operational excellence, and the effectiveness and advancement of your people.

APPENDIX A

MAXIMIZING YOUR
DESIGN RESOURCES

Your company may possess more design talent than you realize.

To lead a design review, to identify the usability problems that stall so many business systems, and to propose solutions all require someone who has multiple skills. Ideally, this person is adept in leadership, proficient in collaboration, capable of objectivity, and able to generate and communicate a range of alternative ideas. Designers are trained to practice these skills, but others within your organization also may be able to effectively gather information and use the findings to develop solutions to some of your chronic software problems. Here's how to identify and maximize these valuable human resources.

CAST A WIDE NET

The most effective design teams include diverse professional experience. Even if you have an information architect and interface designers on staff, other specialists within your rank and file may be able to make valuable contributions to the process of evaluating your current system and redefining your business needs. One of your sales or marketing experts may be more attuned to the needs of the people who use your system than the people who run it, and one of your communications officers should be able to help clarify the messages your system is sending.

The most capable designer in your group may not be the most stylishly dressed man or woman or the creative type who can assemble highly polished PowerPoint presentations. Find out whether anyone on your staff has experience in a profession dedicated to communicating visual information—graphic design, cartography, landscape architecture, or even filmmaking. All these specialties require techniques of observation and problem solving that are basic to the process of good product design.

In choosing someone to take the leadership role in a design review, look for someone who has an inclusive management style as well as strong subject-matter skills. The design process thrives on collaboration, so if your creative director works best alone, don't ask that person to act as liaison between business analysts, technologists, and the people who use the system. A product manager might be a better candidate.

The best candidate will be someone who has extensive experience in problem solving and who knows how to examine a broad range of questions. Designing a successful product requires an appreciation that the challenge extends beyond technology and calls for a capacity to think strategically about the product and to envision it in a larger context—the ways in which it will be used.

ASSESS AUTHORITY

Many software vendors employ vast design teams, and your own internal information technology group may already have individuals focused on these concerns. Unfortunately, these professionals often play second fiddle to business analysts and programming staffers whose attitudes, numbers, and processes (or a combination of these) stifle the voices of in-house design professionals and prevent them from realizing the positive impact they could have on a product during its development.

If your company currently employs interface designers, find out whether they are being given opportunities to work directly with the business side to develop solutions or if they are expected to take orders and deliver precisely according to spec. Do they represent an ineffective checkpoint awkwardly squeezed into an already frenetic software development process? Asking them to share responsibility for proposing solutions can make a dramatic difference.

CONSIDER REALLOCATING YOUR RESOURCES

Some members of your staff may possess design skills that can be redeployed to draft wireframes, screen shots, and other inexpensive prototypes for review and revision by your business specialists.

Managing the budget a bit differently also can make a big impact. If you have a team of software developers on staff, consider that instead of filling your next slot for a programmer—someone to pound away at code—you might hire a design production person who could work with the tech side to draft prototypes, flesh out concepts, and act as a link between technology and the business side.

ANOINT THE STANDARD-BEARER

Once you've identified the person who is best qualified to lead a design review, spread the news. This person must be given the authority to rally the troops throughout the company, explore alternative solutions, and build consensus, so that everyone who is asked to make a contribution will feel responsible for the success of the effort.

The leader of the design review should be responsible for managing all aspects of the process, including observing and interviewing some of the staff members who use your current system, obtaining baseline measurements of the usability of that system, collaborating with technologists to sketch proposed revisions, and taking those drawings around the company, from department to department, to hammer out the details. Make everyone aware that this project is a priority, and that their contributions—if requested—are essential.

GATHER THE METRICS

You can begin to measure the usability of your current system simply by finding out how long it takes six users to perform certain tasks.

Performing a language assessment is another good test of usability, and many tools are available online to show how to perform card-sorting exercises. These tests can detect problem areas by telling you how well the nouns and verbs within your present system correspond to the general understanding of those words in your workplace.

DEVELOP AN ACTION PLAN

Don't mistake usability testing for a genuine focus on design. The purpose of usability testing is to evaluate a product, and its results are meant to inform the refinement of a design.

When the design process influences the definition and development of a new system—who it will serve, what it must do, and how it must do it—usability testing can easily demonstrate whether a proposed design is the optimal solution. But usability testing of an existing application can be helpful only if you have a strategy in place to act on the things that testing may reveal. Miles of office shelves are lined with binders documenting the results of usability testing. These analyses are worthless unless they are followed by action. Imagine if the work of a physician were limited to forming a diagnosis that confirms what you already suspect: "Yes, you are sick."

Once you have a better understanding of how effectively your system performs in the hands of its users and how clearly it communicates with them, you'll have the information you need to diagnose the source of the problems and build a team to design solutions.

APPENDIX B

TOUGH QUESTIONS
FOR CONSULTANTS

You may decide that you need an outside opinion. Even if your company has the capability to produce wireframes and other prototypes, perhaps you need additional resources: a designer who specializes in developing, testing, and validating specifications for software systems, or a consultant who specializes in testing the usability of software.

It's no disgrace not to do it all yourself—many of the world's largest product companies, including Microsoft, routinely outsource design and usability work. If your company has no depth of experience in product design or the study of human behavior, consider adding a specialist to your team. But before you hire a designer, a consulting design company, or a usability expert, ask these questions.

WHAT ARE YOUR SPECIALTIES?

Selecting the correct design leadership from an ocean of consultants can be difficult unless you consider how well a consultant's strength matches your present and future needs.

The lines between many areas of business operations are blurred and are becoming even more fluid. Web sites that once were advertising and marketing venues are now complex, highly transactional business systems, and your company's internal systems may now be running inside a Web browser. Internal systems that are distributed to users through a browser shouldn't be confused with Web sites, and you shouldn't employ creative embellishments to pretty them up—this is not design. Advertising and marketing firms that were excellent partners for the most recent incarnation of your visually compelling Web site may not possess the chops to design the online business system that your next site must become.

If you're interviewing a design consultancy, you will definitely want a partner who knows how software is developed and tested, and how design methods can be elegantly and effectively woven into current software development processes. You also may be seeking specialized expertise in needs assessment, interface design, usability, information architecture, or reconfiguration of software systems. However, if you're interviewing a designer to fill a position on your staff, look for a generalist, someone who has designed solutions to a variety of problems. A skilled designer understands the importance of collaboration and knows how to manage the design process within the realities of production requirements and other business limitations.

WHAT ARE SOME OF THE PROBLEMS YOU'VE SOLVED WITH DESIGN?

A strong track record of solving a diverse range of problems is an excellent predictor of a candidate's success in solving problems at your own firm.

Hearing accounts of case histories, including challenges within industries quite different from your own, will give you insight into how a designer works. If you manage a health care company, a problem in a financial company may seem somewhat familiar even though the details of its resolution may be unrelated to your own business.

The solution itself is less important than the way in which it was developed and tested. Ask for a description of how a solution was discovered, how it was validated, and how the results were measured. Ask about feedback that was received after the solution was implemented. The design process should lead to a product whose success can be demonstrated.

WHAT'S YOUR PROCESS?

The best way to judge design aptitude is to ask what techniques a designer uses to solve problems. A design portfolio tells you very little. It can demonstrate that a designer has been employed, and it also may show that the designer produced a certain outcome—but you can't be sure of that because the concept may have originated elsewhere. A description of the process that was used to arrive at a solution, or a sketchbook that shows intermediate stages, will reveal so much more.

Listen closely for evidence of collaboration. Recently I interviewed a designer who possessed all the skills and experience my company typically seeks, but as we talked it became clear that she had a single-minded vision of the problem-solving process. When I asked about how she works with programmers, the engineers who ultimately build what she designs, her response was, "I like to keep them out of my hair until I'm done." *Wow*, I thought—*that's risky!* Then, when I asked what experience she'd had in working with human factors specialists, she told me, "I know everything they know." Those were two wrong answers. It was obvious that she had no idea of the potential benefits of collaborating with a technologist or a psychologist, and it was hard to imagine her being willing to consider the opinions and experience of a warehouse manager or a customer service rep. Rarely do we work in an environment where all disciplines are equally and effectively represented, so it's important to find out how a designer bridges these gaps.

A designer's success is dependent upon an ability to build consensus. Designers are trained to listen and observe, to gather information, to lead a creative process with a diverse group of individuals, and to orchestrate a cacophony of voices into a rich, clear chorus. A good designer isn't the soloist.

Look for a pattern in the process. When we interview designers for my company, we try to find those who perform a sequence of problem-solving activities again and again before they arrive at a solution. We search for designers who tell us, *I heard someone say this,* or *I saw a need for that*—stories of how other people influenced their ideas. The sequence of steps in the process may vary, and the influences may change from project to project, but we look for designers who talk about the ways in which their work has been informed by the people around them. That's how we hire a designer.

HOW WOULD YOU GO ABOUT SOLVING OUR PROBLEM?

A good design consultant will describe a process rather than a solution. Distinguish between identifying the problem, developing a solution, and implementing the solution.

Whatever your immediate problem with your software system, make sure that the designer's focus is broader than technology, because designing a solution may be more challenging than implementing it. In fact, modifying the technology could be the most straightforward part of the process.

It's probable that the solution will require some reconfiguration of your system—tweaking the code, rearranging the sequence of screen views, or reorganizing data on the screen—but it may be possible to do this work in-house in collaboration with a design consultant who sets the direction and writes the specifications. Implementation also may be done by a third-party technology partner.

Whether design consultants develop a proposal for action or implement technical solutions in partnership with their clients, they provide real value only when they contribute specialized design expertise—a process that supplements and builds on the knowledge of business and technology with a fresh perspective and objective advice.

NOTES

Source notes are listed by page number and by a phrase or quotation on that page.

ONE IT'S JUST A PRODUCT!

2   After a 10-year global survey: "2004 Third Quarter Research Report," The Standish Group International, Inc. (West Yarmouth, MA: Standish Group, 2004).

3   $13 billion: Gartner Inc., "Market Trends: Application Development, Worldwide, 2008–2013," Laurie F. Wurster et al. (Stamford, CT: Gartner Inc., January 30, 2009).

6   $149 billion: Tim Miles, "Software Industry Data," Office of Technology and Electronic Commerce, Manufacturing and Services (Washington, D.C.: U.S. Department of Commerce, February 2009).

7   Morgan Stanley: Reuters, February 7, 2007.

7   Hershey: Wendy Tanaka, "Hershey's Inventory Computer Problems Thing of the Past," *Philadelphia Inquirer,* November 1, 2002.

7   Invacare: Invacare Corporation, news release, February 16, 2006. www.invacare.com/cgi-bin/imhqprd/inv_news/newsArticleOnly.jsp?s=0&passedChildOID=537121761.

7   emergency dispatch system: Charlie White, "Computer Glitch Turns 911 Calls into Headache for Dispatchers," *Courier-Journal* (Louisville, KY), November 8, 2005, Metro Edition, B5.

7   air-traffic control center: Jennifer Oldham, "FAA to Probe Radio Failure," *Los Angeles Times,* September 17, 2004, Metro Edition, B3.

8   air-traffic control center: Ibid.

8   Veterans Administration: Hope Yen, Associated Press, "Records: Vets Given Incorrect Doses," *Boston Globe,* January 15, 2009.

8    $59.5 billion: NIST Planning Report 02-3, "The Economic Impacts of Inadequate Infrastructure for Software Testing" (Washington, D.C.: National Institute of Standards and Technology, Department of Commerce, June 2002).

13   MP1: Olivetti Telecom Italia S.p.A. www.olivetti.nu/history.htm.

14   Olivetti: Ibid.

14   This handsome machine: "Modernist Dreams, 4 Case Studies: Ivrea," Modern Movement (MoMo) Neighbourhood Cooperation (Sunila, Finland: an EU Culture 2000 Project). http://momoneco.kotka.fi/ivrea_nayttely_2_uk.html.

14   New models: Olivetti Telecom Italia S.p.A. www.olivetti.nu/history.htm.

15   Nearly 70 years later, Apple Computer: Leander Kahney, "Inside Look at Birth of the iPod," *Wired,* July 21, 2004.

TWO DESIGN TO DELIGHT

23   "who we might ideally be": Alain de Botton, *The Architecture of Happiness* (New York: Vintage International, 2006), 3.

30   Forrester Research: Jennifer Chew with Laurie M. Orlov and Liz Herbert, "App User Interfaces Still Need Work," Forrester Research, Inc., January 8, 2003. www.forrester.com/ER/Research/Brief/Excerpt/0,1317,16184,00.html.

THREE SPECIFY INNOVATION

60   Moen Incorporated: William C. Taylor, "Get Out of That Rut and into the Shower," *New York Times,* August 13, 2006, Business, 5.

66   One April evening: Pat Moore with Charles Paul Conn, *Disguised, a True Story* (Waco, TX: Word Books, 1985), 18.

66   Patricia Moore and Raymond Loewy: Ibid., 12–13.

67 "Dutch": Ibid., 13.

67 "Look at my face": Ibid., 19.

67 disguise: Ibid., 23, 55, 56, 57, 174.

67 Seven years later: Walter Nicholls, "Getting a Grip: How OXO Invented Hand-Friendly Kitchen Tools," *Washington Post*, October 17, 1999.

68 one that would quickly need to be replaced: Ibid.

68 He realized that nearly every utensil: Christopher Palmeri, "I Need to Be Making and Selling Things," *Forbes*, February 17, 1992.

68 Smart Design employed designers: "Sam Farber's Back in Business," *HFD, The Weekly Home Furnishings Newspaper*, April 23, 1990.

68 By this time Patricia Moore's company: Mary Vespa, "Designer Pat Moore Learned about Old Age the Hard Way," *Time*, June 24, 1985.

68 To Smart Design, her firm looked like a natural fit: Bruce Nussbaum, "What Works for One Works for All," *BusinessWeek*, April 20, 1992.

68 Working together: "Sam Farber's Back in Business," *HFD*.

68 OXO, a name: Nicholls, "Getting a Grip."

68 he was confident: "Sam Farber's Back in Business," *HFD*.

69 "I have never come up with a more meaningful product": Ibid.

69 $750,000: Palmeri, "I Need to Be Making and Selling Things."

69 $273 million: "Helen of Troy Limited Completes OXO International Acquisition," PR Newswire, June 2, 2004.

FOUR CONSIDER THE CONSEQUENCES

72 in 1863: "Public Transport in Victorian London, Part Two: Underground," London Transport Museum. www.ltmcollection.org/resources/index.html? IXglossary=Public+transport+in+Victorian+London%.

72 serving 255 stations: Douglas Alexander, Secretary of State for Transport, "Progress of the London Underground and National Railways Security Studies," statement to Parliament, March 15, 2007. www.dft.gov.uk/ press/speechesstatements/statements/railwayssecurity.

72 Harry Beck: "Harry Beck's Iconic Map," Icons. A Portrait of England. www.icons.org.uk/theicons/collection/the-tube-map/biography/ harry-beck-s-revolutionary-map.

74   Beck: Ibid.

78   Accounting Software Advisor: ASA Research, Accounting Software Advisor, L.L.C. www.asaresearch.com/articles/implement.htm.

91   Gartner, Inc.: "Gartner Says Eight of Ten Dollars Enterprises Spend on IT Is 'Dead Money,'" Gartner, Inc., October 9, 2006. www.gartner.com/it/page.jsp?id=497088.

92   "health care in the United States": Linda T. Kohn, Janet Corrigan, and Molla S. Donaldson, eds., "To Err Is Human: Building a Safer Health System," Committee on Quality of Health Care in America, Institute of Medicine (Washington, D.C.: National Academies Press, 2000).

93   the report stated: Ibid.

93   The Leapfrog Group: "The Business Roundtable Launches Effort to Help Reduce Medical Errors through Purchasing Power Clout," press release, The Leapfrog Group, November 15, 2000. www.leapfroggroup.org/media/file/Leapfrog-Launch-Press_Release.pdf.

93   Three years later, Children's Hospital of Pittsburgh: "Children's Hospital of Pittsburgh Names New Chief Medical Information Officer to Lead Implementation of Digital System," news release, Children's Hospital of Pittsburgh, October 4, 2006. www.chp.edu/CHP/100406.

94   The hospital's computerized order entry system: Lynne Glover, "Electronic Order-Entry System at Children's Hospital Aims to Reduce Rate of Medical Error," *Pittsburgh Business Times*, June 6, 2003.

94   Children'sNet went live: "Children's Hospital of Pittsburgh Unveils High-Tech Computer System for Patient Records and Physician Orders," news release, Children's Hospital of Pittsburgh, December 10, 2002. www.chp.edu/CHP/121002.

94   "Even the most foolproof verbal and manual processes": Ibid.

94   "a prescription for accuracy": Luis Fabregas, "A Prescription for Accuracy," *Pittsburgh Tribune-Review,* December 11, 2002.

94   In an article for *Pediatrics*: Yong Y. Han, M.D., et al., "Unexpected Increased Mortality after Implementation of a Commercially Sold Computerized Physician Order Entry System," *Pediatrics* 116, no. 6 (December 2005): 1506–1512.

95   Not only: Ibid.

96   *with the latter*: Ibid.

FIVE THE RIGHT TEAM

104 "appeared to settle under the surface like a submarine": Stanley N. Roscoe, "From the Roots to the Branches of Cockpit Design: Problems, Principles, Products," *Human Factors Society Bulletin* 35, no. 12 (Santa Monica, CA: Human Factors and Ergonomics Society, 1992).

104 Alphonse Chapanis: Ibid.

105 Chapanis realized: Ibid.

105 engineering psychology: Stanley N. Roscoe, *The Adolescence of Engineering Psychology*, Human Factors History Monograph Series 1, Steven M. Casey, ed. (Santa Monica, CA: Human Factors and Ergonomics Society, 1997).

105 Human Factors Society of America: The Human Factors and Ergonomics Society. www.hfes.org/web/AboutHFES/history.html.

SIX FIND OUT WHAT YOU REALLY NEED

140 Toyota: www.mccarthylexus.co.za/news.cfm?ipkSiteMenuLinkID=7&detail=56.

141 Lexus: Ibid.

NINE YOUR NEXT SYSTEM

197 Waste Management, Inc.: Mary Hayes Weier, "SAP Software a 'Complete Failure,' Lawsuit Claims," *InformationWeek,* March 27, 2008.

198 charged that SAP: Ibid.

ILLUSTRATION CREDITS

36   © iStockphoto.com/Steve Brodie.

37   Courtesy of www.stpetersbasilica.org.

41   Athenaeum of Philadelphia.

43   (*top left*) Library of Congress, Prints and Photographs Division, Historic American Buildings Survey/Historic American Engineering Record, HABS WIS,51-RACI,5-21. (*top right*) Library of Congress, Prints and Photographs Division, HABS WIS,51-RACI,5-18. (*bottom, left and right*) © 2009 Bloomberg Finance L.P. All rights reserved. Used with permission.

52   (*left*) Detail of sketch © 2009 Frank Lloyd Wright Foundation, AZ/Art Resource, NY/Artists Rights Society (ARS), NY. (*right*) Archive Timothy McCarthy/Art Resource, NY.

54   Detail of photograph © Roy Export SAS.

55   (*left*) Library of Congress, Prints and Photographs Division, National Child Labor Committee Collection, LC-DIG-nclc-01358. (*right*) Library of Congress, Prints and Photographs Division, LC-DIG-nclc-01830.

67   (*top*) © Hemera Technologies/PhotoObjects.net/Jupiterimages.com. (*bottom*) Courtesy of OXO.

69   Courtesy of OXO.

70   © James Smith/GreatBuildings.com.

72   © TfL, from the London Transport Museum collection.

73   © TfL, from the London Transport Museum collection.

74   (*left*) Courtesy of © WMATA. (*right*) Tokyo Metro Co. Ltd © 2008.6.

98   Photographs and logo provided courtesy of Carnegie Mellon University.

99   (*top*) Image copyright © Gail Johnson, 2009. Used under license from Shutterstock.com. (*bottom*) Courtesy of IBM Corporate Archives.

103   U.S. Air Force photo/National Museum of the United States Air Force.

104   U.S. Air Force photo/National Museum of the United States Air Force.

105   U.S. Air Force photo/National Museum of the United States Air Force.

106   (*top*) Image copyright © Scott Rothstein, 2009. Used under license from Shutterstock.com. (*bottom*) Courtesy of Target.

109   © Harold Hambrose.

127   © Eric C. Lindstrom.

129 © Eric C. Lindstrom.

130 © Eric C. Lindstrom.

134 Courtesy of Lucasfilm Ltd. *Raiders of the Lost Ark*™ & © 1981 Lucasfilm Ltd. All rights reserved. Used under authorization. Unauthorized duplication is a violation of applicable law.

136 Reproduced courtesy of Rohm and Haas Company © 2006.

138 Detail of hobo symbols on sign, photo by Infrogmation, http://creativecommons.org/licenses/by/2.5/.

140 The Lexus name and logo are registered trademarks of Toyota Motor Corporation.

143 (*left*) Image copyright © Neale Cousland, 2009. Used under license from Shutterstock.com. (*right*) Image copyright © Orpheus, 2009. Used under license from Shutterstock.com.

144 Matt Wargo, courtesy Venturi, Scott Brown and Associates, Inc.

145 Matt Wargo, courtesy Venturi, Scott Brown and Associates, Inc.

147 Reproduced courtesy of PJM Interconnection © 2007.

150 © Spencer J. Schimel, Carnegie Mellon University, School of Design.

151 © Benjamin Wojtyna.

153 © Siegfried Layda/The Image Bank/Getty Images.

164 Detail of photograph courtesy of Universal Studios Licensing LLLP; The Kobal Collection.

165 Detail of photograph courtesy of Universal Studios Licensing LLLP; The Kobal Collection.

170 © Harold Hambrose.

171 © Harold Hambrose.

179 © iStockphoto/Mikhail Kokhanchikov.

181 © Media Bakery.

182 © iStockphoto.com/MidwestWilderness.

190 © iStockphoto.com/Cassandra Tiensivu.

192 © iStockphoto.com/mustafa deliormanli.

195 © Popperfoto/Getty Images.

INDEX

Page numbers of illustrations are printed in *italics*.